MIXED MUSINGS

Edited by

Andrew Head

First published in Great Britain in 1997 by
POETRY NOW
1-2 Wainman Road, Woodston,
Peterborough, PE2 7BU
Telephone (01733) 230746
Fax (01733) 230751

All Rights Reserved

Copyright Contributors 1997

HB ISBN 1 86188 527 X
SB ISBN 1 86188 522 9

FOREWORD

Although we are a nation of poetry writers we are accused of not reading poetry and not buying poetry books: after many years of listening to the incessant gripes of poetry publishers, I can only assume that the books they publish, in general, are books that most people do not want to read.
Poetry should not be obscure, introverted, and as cryptic as a crossword puzzle: it is the poet's duty to reach out and embrace the world.
The world owes the poet nothing and we should not be expected to dig and delve into a rambling discourse searching for some inner meaning.
The reason we write poetry (and almost all of us do) is because we want to communicate: an ideal; an idea; or a specific feeling. Poetry is as essential in communication, as a letter; a radio; a telephone, and the main criteria for selecting the poems in this anthology is very simple: they communicate.
This is a poetry anthology which holds over 100 poems covering many different topics. It's a representation of the standard of poetry which is being written by today's poets.
The poetry is written by all different types of people yet all of them have a passion for poetry. People write poetry for various reasons for some it's just a hobby, for others it's a way of expressing their thoughts, but for whatever reason, it is always an excellent form of communication. Poetry is uninterrupted and you can express your opinions and views exactly as you want them to be heard. And that's why *Mixed Musings* is a special anthology; containing honest and truthful feelings and thoughts which give a true insight into the people of today.

Contents

When Goodbye Is The Only Answer	Neil Adrian Fisher	1
Conversation At Fortnum And Mason	G E Khandelwal	1
Spring Has Come Again	Justin Shaw	2
A Little Whisper	J E Hill	3
The Old Way	L A Churchill	4
Anger	Penqin	4
Youth Of Today!	Mary Wood	5
Sisters	A J Moulson	6
Wind	Anne Melling	7
Sunset	Christine Flowers	8
The Buttonhole	George Pearson	9
Silent Hill	Shona King	9
The Twelfth Of July	Paul Harvey Jackson	10
The Horrors Of War	Joyce Kempton	11
All Men Are Fools	Philip Addyman	12
Father	Sarah-Helen Stewart	13
First Love	Margaret George	14
Only You!	Katie Luckes	15
Eva	Yvonne Monks	16
I Tried So Hard	J Danson	17
Changes	Jon Morris	18
Safe Embrace	Barbara J Parsons	19
In Sweet Accord	Ann Merryweather	19
For You	Sarah Field	20
The Cave	Hannah Bakewell	20
Nature In All Her Glory	Sylvia Fear Parkinson	21
Today	G W Bailey	21
Is Everything Made Of Plastic?	Steven Cannings	22
A Coastal Walk	Elizabeth Hunter	23
Nature	Paul Secrett	24
My First And Only Love	Eileen Kyte	25
As The Bells Ring	Jacqueline D Rhodes	26
The Dovecote	Dorothy Brookes	27

The True Me	Clive Cornwall	28
Message From Holst	Anne Savan	29
The Homecoming 1987	Claude A Knight	30
Who Is There?	Barbara Ramsay	31
Alone With Prayer	K Kay	32
Alone	Ann P Tilt	32
The Driving Test	W O Z Warwick	33
My Riverside Walk	Helen Crawford	34
One Broken Heart For Sale	Leigh Smart	35
Jed The Farmhand And His Broken Heart	Alex I Askaroff	36
Resolved	Brian Hemming	37
Love?	Aleksandra Tutus	38
Beauty In Bleakness	Dawn Madigan	39
A Child's Love	Mo Lyon	40
A Silent Song	Brian Casson	41
Love	Evelyn Ida Henfield	42
Love	Stanley W Croxtall	43
Absent Friends	Tess Whitlock	43
January Stream	Victoria Schofield	44
New Birth Of Spring	Mary Hulme	44
A Time For Every Season	Janet Hewitt	45
New Year Celebrations Of A Baby Elephant	Andrew Baily	46
Jesus Christ	David Stockdale	46
True Love	Doris Davis	47
A Pigeon's Nest	The Painter In Words	48
Archie	Lara Higgins	48
A Goodnight Kiss	Wayne & Christine Devlin	49
A Pint Of Dreams	Kevin Turner	49
Snowflake	Patricia Woodley	50
A New Year	L A Brown	51
It's Like This	Ronald Stanley Unsworth	52
The Last Resolution	Francis Marshall	53
Where Am I	Stephanie Waller	53
Wheels	Maureen Lucas	54
Love	Helga Morris	55

First Love	Deborah Baker	56
What Is Love?	Rex Taylor	57
You're All I'll Ever Need	Adam Griffiths	58
The Whispering Breeze	Joan Hands	59
A New Leaf	David Bridgewater	60
Why-Why-Why?	Olive Wright	61
Jabs	Gilda Ward	62
She Came To Me	Susan Goldsmith	63
Autumn	Patricia Haynes	64
What It Means To Me	L Futia	64
A Donkey's Day Out	Charlotte Sainsbury	65
Special Day	T J M Walker	66
Someday	Leanne Victoria Buck	66
God's Work - His Wonders To Perform	Bruce Ward	67
Fidelity	Julian Matthews	67
Priceless Treasure	Esther Rehill	68
Tree House	Julie Ashpool	69
Assurance	John Henry Bridgeman	70
The Feast Of The Turnover	Laurence Keen	71
The Song Of The Dolphins	Solomon Blue Waters	72
The Village	R S Hooper	72
The Gifts Of God	Joyce M Turner	73
Back To Eden!	Mary Skelton	74
Mountains	Tony Jones	75
The Poor Old Polar Bear	Kerry Bennett	75
Love's Saga	Laurence Parfitt	76
Moved Away	C Rodrigues	76
Newness Of Life	Jane Stagg	77
False Witness	John Carter-Dolman	78
Faith	Lee Ryder	79
The Heavenly Saviour	Stephanie Bones	80
You Are Welcome	Jean Lloyd-Williams	81
In My Thoughts	Kathleen Hurlow	82
At War (The Bombing Raid)	C Parry	83
What's Past Is Past	D Eales	84
Bitterness At The Terminal	Jenny Clarkson	85

Phone Box	Vickie Simpson	85
Suspended Animation	Deana Houghton	86
The Routine	Chris Antcliff	87
Sounds	Wendy Nobbs	88
Retiring In The Country	Joan Britton	89
Junkie	Vanessa Fitzgerald	89
Love	Sadie R Flather	90
Too Much	Gerard Phillips	91
Gulls	Edward Colson	91
Something For Nothing	Steve McIlroy	92
Mind-Warp Factor Ten	Chris Hails	93
Joe, Stephanie And Cheriée	Donna Jamison	94
The Ka	Patricia M Sharp	95
Thief Of Time	John Mallows	96
The School Governor	Donald Jay	97
The Dear Garden	Katherine Smart	98
Katy	Linda J Proom	99
Dare To Dream	Norman Wright	100
8 Hours A Day	P J Gassner	101
Coming To The End Of Life's Journey	P Wright	102
The Old Antique Dealer, My Friend	Leila Maryat	103
Ode To Alanna	Magdalene McKinney	104
Hurt	J M Lerigo	105
The Flying Vet	Hilary J Hulford	106
Karaoke Queen (Not)	Delia Bennett	107
In My Thoughts	M E Smith	108
No Time To Stop	Amii Rowlinson	109
Machine And Man	Rita Humphrey	109
Groan And Mumble	Joyce Mason	110
Forever Friends	Sandra Pocock	111
Life On The Street	Ernest Hall	112
The Morning After The Night Before	Lee Silvera	113
You	Pauline Bell	114
Stargazers	Saleha Chowdhury	115

Inseparable	Rogan Whitenails	116
Gulf Conflict	J W McCarthy	117
In My Thoughts	Julie Holmes	118
Life In The Fast Lane	Gwyneth M Glascodine	119
The Illicit Dram	Janet Boulton	120
The Refuge	Nellie Heard	121
The Morning After	Finé Buliciri	122
After All The Months	Patricia Cook	123
I Wake Alone	Karen Hutton	124
For David Holbrook	Stan Downing	124
Times Past	Helen Kempt	125
Dedicated To My Friend	Marjorie Doris Walshe	126
What's A Few Thousand Miles Between Friends?	Linda Bagnall	127
Obstruction On The Motorway	Audrey Woodall	128
Light Up A Light	Mary Jo West	129
Dream Giver	Doreen King	130
Missing Ewe	Naomi Engelkamp	131
In My Thoughts	Irene Elliot	132
Winter Ploughing	Margaret Baxter	133
The Final Release	Melanie Jane Banner	134
RGM	Tim Hart	135
One Night, Last Night	Jacky Hartley	136
A One 'Knight' Stand	Pim Foster	137
Apopletic!	J A Wright	138
My Long Lost Cousin	Susan Forrest	139
Choices	Angela Watson	140
Condolences	Carole Wallis	140
Shoreline	Stephen Gyles	141
Brown Study	Barbara Turner	142
Seasons	Joyce Boast	143
First Love	M Cook	144
Missing Out	Jayne Hempstock	145
An Immigrant's Farewell	David B Small	146
An Acquired Taste	Tess Thomas	147
Last Night Of The Poms	Alan McAlpine Douglas	148

Sunday Night	Marda Day	149
Absent Memories	Allen Meade	150
Kathleen	John Hopper	151
Renewal	Joyce Barbara	152
Mutual Love	Scott Poulter	153
Night Flight	Andrew Kerr	154
The Rebel	Sheila Ellen Wright	155
Battersea Park	Valerie Dawson	156
Family Ties	Jeanne Ellmore	157
Dwelling On A One Night Stand	Kerry Brady	158
Friendship Straight And True	Doreen Ranson	159

WHEN GOODBYE IS THE ONLY ANSWER

Why do I have to ask your name,
When only I want to know my name.
Why do I have to seek out the ring on your finger,
When trust cannot be weighed in gold alone.
Why do I need to know if you were the one taking precautions,
When you know that accidents can play no part in the future.
Why must I only guess what you write in your diary,
When my today, may depend on your yesterday.
Why can I allow regret only to last until breakfast,
When I can only guess if you prefer tea or coffee.
Why am I asking these questions,
When the answer is always going to be goodbye.

Neil Adrian Fisher

CONVERSATION AT FORTNUM AND MASON

'Have you been skiing yet this year?'
'We've been to Cloisters as usual dear.'
'Are you going to Scotland for the shoot?'
'Oh yes, shooting grouse is such a hoot.'
'Have you dealt with that new stockbroker?'
'He suggested Lloyds, oh what a joker!'
'We're flying down to Cannes next week.'
'Oh we're off to the Island of Mustique.'
'Is your daughter coming out at the debutantes' ball?'
'Yes, and I don't think she'll be a flower at the wall.'
'Have you your hat for Royal Ascot yet?'
'Yes, it's really smart and covered with net.'
'Have you read that new book called Wild Swan?'
'Yes, but it made me feel, ever so wan.'
'I must dash now, or I'm going to be late.
I'm having tea at the Ritz, with my friend Kate.'

G E Khandelwal

SPRING HAS COME AGAIN
(Dedicated to Charlotte Milloy, ever been confused by love?)

The year slowly draws one.
Only three long months to go.
But, autumn and winter haven't come,
I am not sad, not to see them.
Spring has taken its toll,
And come twice this year.

I sit by the fireside, untouched by the heat.
This October isn't cold,
At last after these icy three
Long, long years,
The stars have brought upon me,
Hope, thank God, I am lucky.
After this eternity, I have won.
Spring has come along.

Justin Shaw

A LITTLE WHISPER

A little whisper I love you
Is all we need to hear
To fill our lives with happiness
And take away our fears.

Just those words, those words alone
Are all we need or seek
There's many that can say them
But others are too weak.

Love is deep within us all
For everyone to share
It's a word that is so precious
So why do some not care?

A little whisper I love you
Is a word we can all treasure
For when said by a loved one
We remember it forever.

Just those words, those words alone
A little whisper I love you
To the people that we care for
Should be said, but should be true.

Love is what God gave us all
So that we could all share
A little love in life on earth
So why not show we care.

J E Hill

THE OLD WAY

See this idle waterway,
The ducks, the stone bridge . . .

and over it steams an engine
fast, black with hot power. The rails

taking the load and doing
the work. Then look,

see the road, built along
now where the tracks used to stride:

rushing, busy with directed
lives. Then look boyo, again,

they're cleaning the channel, so
we can go by boat, quiet, the old way.

L A Churchill

ANGER

I feel anger when I see the
injustices of this world.
being taken out on the
working classes
of this country and they
are blamed for all the
ills in the world.
But if it was not for the
 masses where would
the 'fat cat' politicans be . . .?
        Out of business!

Penqin

YOUTH OF TODAY!

The youth walked purposefully into the corner shop
Earring dangling and shaved hair crop
Tattooed, with nose-stud shining bright
Enough to give decent folk a fright!

Warily, the assistant watched as he approached
She was serving a pensioner when he encroached
He looked at the lady and cheekily declared
'Hurry up granny!' The assistant glared!

'How dare you speak to my customer that way
There is no respect from the youth of today!
You wait your turn, as you always should
To be rude to people will do you no good!'

The pensioner, unable to believe her ears
Could not understand the assistant's jeers
Bemused, she said, 'Now have you done?
I *am* his granny - he's my daughter's son!'

Mary Wood

SISTERS

I have a very dear sister
who I love so very much,
she is so kind and gentle
and very soft to touch.

Her word can say and mean so much
he love's so warm to handle,
her heart is made of purest gold
and her eyes sparkle like a candle.

I love my sister very much
and I know she loves me too,
why can't I say the words I want to hear
it seems so hard to do.

A rose I'd like to give to her
to tell her how I feel,
the words would make my life complete
and my love for her so real.

A J Moulson

WIND

Probing the cracks and crevices
Like a lover's tongue.
Punishing the light and gentle
Like a hairdresser teasing a new style.
Battering tiles and plaster
Like a ram at a buttress.
Teasing the cobwebs and litter
Like a lion salivating at prey.
Screaming through the keyhole
Like a new-born baby in delivery.
Caressing branches and leaves
Like a mother stroking a child's head.
Carrying debris and clutter
Like a miner carrying a comrade.
Chilling the voyageur
Like ice, freezing meat in the ice-box.

Destructive - like a tornado in a haystack.
Cooling - like a lemonade in summer.
Endless - like the outer limits of Space.

Wind-blowing its own trumpet!

Anne Melling

SUNSET

Spherical burnt orange hung over
the flat escarpment of day.
Cold, silvery and grey fish-like particles
fragmented the lake below,
Drifting sporadically like feathers
rippling against the water's edge.
Daylight disappeared slowly like a
thief in the night.
Its residual legacy resounding into
a fanciful flight of colour, texture and hue.
Woven into a thick velvety tapestry
rationed only by darkness;
Nature coloured my eye as this
burning blaze of colour
Sunk deeper into the horizon
towards the close of day.
The giant saucer-like sunset
descended quickly into oblivion.

Christine Flowers

The Buttonhole

Four upon the boulevard, arm in arm and cosy.
Pick a flower for every one
and one shall be for Rosie.

One azalea for Jill, two for Meg and Josie,
but a secret, silent gem
especially for Rosie.

Four walk on the boulevard fingering their posy,
every petal bears a loan
of love intent on Rosie.

One azalea for Jill, two for Meg and Josie,
as along one special stem
run messengers to Rosie.

George Pearson

Silent Hill

Come listen, listen, can you hear it still
a faintful cry, just over the hill
a lonely man so frail and thin
the pain so strong and coming within
help me, help me he sighs in sin
the war is over and no-one can win
reach for my hand and I'll show you the way
come back and ask me one lonely day
was it a dream or did I say
an angel, an angel God has sent her my way.

Shona King

THE TWELFTH OF JULY

In Ulster the twelfth's a quare aul' joke for some
But for loyal Orangemen 'tis serious business
                        celebrating who won
Twelfth of July 1690 was a victory for 'Prods'
Over the 'taigs' of King James all batttling the odds.

Sure the Battle of the Boyne ended in rout
When James and his troops had to 'cop out'
Leaving King Billy the victor for ever and a day
That's why the twelfth will permanently stay.

So when Willy John from Armagh dons bowler and sash
To walk with his Lodge he cuts a right dash
Each year on the twelfth he parades with his mates
To the field to eat stew from enormous tin plates.

He'll swagger the best to the skirl of the pipes
Behind a pipe major with an armful of stripes
To listen to speeches; to see folk of all class
Perhaps help his stiff limbs with the aid of a glass.

On the long journey home he'll cough and he'll wheeze
For his feet'll be near paralysed up to his knees
Whether it's rain or it's snow he'll be only too happy
Never will he feel his special day is crappy.

No matter the weather whatever aul' buck
There'll be a smile on his face that looks if it's stuck
For Willy John knows the blood in his veins is not red
Sure it's pure orange juice from his toes to his head!

Paul Harvey Jackson

THE HORRORS OF WAR

Buildings burn, people cry
Bodies all around, many will die
Children bewildered big sad eyes
Guns being fired, more lost lives

The fear in the faces of the young and old
Devastation all around, no protection
from the cold,
Mummy, mummy, a child wails,
His mummy died when the last bomb fell.

Hospitals full, power down
Medication low, doctor's battle on.
We hope that aid will soon arrive
To give doctors hope in saving lives.

The horrors of war we are all aware
For those affected we say a prayer

We pray dear God, soon there will be Peace,
hope and harmony.
In this country so ravaged by war
Silence the guns and peace restore.

Joyce Kempton

ALL MEN ARE FOOLS

All men are fools.
They'd kill the gaze
Of treasured jewels
To set their loins
On fire again.

All men have fears.
They've stumbled with
A crippled tongue,
Each eighty years
Since vicious young.

All men they crave.
The purest love
Or diamond heart
Could not deter
This yearning slave.

All men they know.
Each setting sun
Their power grows,
Each future plays
Their waiting game.

All men are fools.
They'd listen but
Their history rules
To nurture their
Inherent claims.

All men are fools.
Behind their pride
Salvation lies,
Outside their heart
Emotion dies.

Philip Addyman

FATHER

My favourite view in all the world,
Is that from on the hill,
Although I moved south long ago,
That picture's with me still.
To drive back towards home again,
Fills me with joy and cheer,
As once I turn into the lane,
I know that you are near.
You're there if I should ever need,
A friend or just a chat,
You have the knack to make me laugh,
I'm very glad of that.
Although we may not talk too much,
I hope you know the score.
You are my father and I know,
I could not love you more.
Remember I am always here,
If you feel down or sad,
For after all you know you are,
My one and only Dad!

Sarah-Helen Stewart

First Love

And do you still remember me
And the golden days long gone
When life was love and love was all
And you and I were young?

Sometimes perhaps a snatch of song
May make you pause and smile
At half-forgotten memories
For just a little while.

And sometimes does a stranger's face
Bring my face to your mind?
A look, a glance, is all it needs
To take you back in time.

And do you ever stop and think
How different life might be
If kindlier fates had smiled on us
And you were still with me?

And me? I found another love
More lasting and more true,
But please sometimes remember me
As I remember you.

Margaret George

ONLY YOU!

*(Thank you for all your love and hugs over the past two years . . .
I love you Brucey)*

Loving, caring tender
That's you through and through
Charming, thoughtful luscious
Is what I think of you.
Your kisses in the morning
Your hugs you give at night
I feel so safe and loved
When you come and hold me tight
Looking in those big blue eyes
My heart begins to dance
The love that I could ever give
Is something you enhance
Your curvaceous body lies
Entwined around my skin
Tempting hands explore
And my mind begins to sin
Sexy thoughts envelop me
My hormones start to roar
You feel my body burning
As you tease me more and more
As I hold you in my arms
I cherish how I feel
You've shown me how to love
A love that is so real
I love you from my heart
Adore you from my soul
Forever I will honour you
My heart and love you stole.

Katie Luckes

Eva

Off to the garden centre, my husband and I,
A small shrub for the garden we wanted to buy
Two years previous his mum had died,
We all loved her so, and how we cried
We thought a tree in the garden would grow
Something delicate with a flowering show
In the front garden we buried it deep
All through the winter it did sleep
The following spring, the beginning of May
It opened its buds, a beautiful display
The leaves all soft a pinky brown,
Soft delicate flowers just like down
As we look at those flowers in full bloom
We smile and think of her, no sign of gloom
Remembering her just as she was
Always helping in a good cause
Small and delicate, gentle and good
God bless you mother-in-law
                    in heaven above.

Yvonne Monks

I Tried So Hard

I looked for all the do's and don'ts,
I felt there should be some.
I tried so hard with my will and wont's
Since Jesus bid me come.

I wanted so much Him to please,
As if I could pay Him back.
And often for kingdom increase,
I'd appear to be on the attack.

I didn't wear trousers for a start,
And threw away my make-up,
But it was what was in my heart,
That was really needing a shake-up.

It didn't matter that my hair wasn't long,
Nor that I didn't wear a head-cover.
There was no merit in being strong,
Nor, for being better than another.

The first is last, the last is first,
You must esteem your brother,
Give drink to all who thirst,
Never put yourself before another.

For this commandment is from above,
'Love one another, as I have loved you.'
When His commandment is to love,
Well, that's what you must do.

J Danson

CHANGES

So, the times have changed and once again, I sit here facing tomorrow's world.
The spirits which have haunted me through an eternity of self doubt have finally shown their faces.
No longer can their unseen presence torment me.
For having seen them,
I realise, now, that my fear came not from the spirits themselves
But from their whispers which echoed menacingly from the darkness.

Yet their words told the truth.
Truth which grazed my soul like the bitter winter winds which burn my skin.
No more must I let the chains of the past imprison my future.
I must throw off the demons.
The autumn leaves which have covered my world must be swept from my life if I am to
receive a spring.
I need a new path, the strength to proceed and a clear way forward to a new world.

Jon Morris

Safe Embrace

When I was small,
I'd fall asleep upon my parents' bed
And dad would come and lift me gently up
And take me to my own.

Then I'd look up through sleepy eyes
And see such tenderness upon his face
As full of love, his kindly eyes smiled down
And I was happy in his safe embrace.

So when you held me gently in your arms last night
And you smiled down in love as you held close to me,
Then drowsily into me crept that warm safe glow,
And once again I was the child I used to be.

Barbara J Parsons

In Sweet Accord

When from the depths of night you came to meet me
our separate dreams combined
and our bodies locked in sweet accord
to make a partnership of heart and sex.

Sleep drenched, we caroused on that wild sea's incoming tide
until moved with desire
to a swelling wave we rose
our bodies cresting to the high pinnacle
and then down below
into a warmly frothing pool of love and sleep
all need washed from us
like storm tossed shingle from a sandy shore.

Ann Merryweather

For You

I know I'll never hear your voice,
I'll never see your face,
But my mind likes to wander
And my heart likes to chase.

I could dream a thousand dreams of you
But it would do no good.
I don't want to forget you,
Although I know I should.

A memory is all I have,
But at a photo' I can stare,
And if I close my eyes for long enough
I see you standing there.

I feel I'm at a dead end
And I don't know what to do.
The only thing I know
Is that I'm in love with you.

Sarah Field (16)

The Cave

The cave was secret and melancholy too
I saw a shadow but it wasn't you.
A crab crawled across the ground,
The noise I heard was big and round.
An echo repeated round the cave,
It sounded like a boastful wave.
A bat swooped down near my head,
Out of the cave into a sunset red.

Hannah Bakewell

NATURE IN ALL HER GLORY

The miracle of nature never ceases to amaze -
The eagle soaring high above while we can only gaze
In wonder. Fish of brilliant coloured hue live among the waves,
While underneath on coloured reefs minute creatures saved
By their host from turtles, whales, and other creatures vast,
So many times their actual size, we would be aghast!
Myriad patterned butterflies among the insect throng
Flocking round the pollened blooms all the summer long.
And down among the woodland, the creatures in their holes -
The rabbits, badgers, weasels, stoats, and furry little voles
Which scamper to the stream's edge, all glistening in the sun,
They all have their place in life, and their place is won
By hunting and alertness - their ears and noses stronger far
Than human ones - we think *we* are the greatest - that belief a bar
To learning how much more there is to know of things around us -
So many deaf and blind to all that does surround us . . .

Sylvia Fear Parkinson

TODAY

Don't waste today, it's very rare,
Try to use it with a care.
Bring a smile to someone's face,
Make the world a better place.

It costs you nothing just to give,
A friendly smile, and help to live.
So offer help where're you go,
'cos you never really know,
How little time you've got to play,
Before the sun sets, on today.

G W Bailey

Is Everything Made Of Plastic?

Life to me seems so sarcastic
I'm living in a world of drastic plastic
Everything is covered with a plastic sleeve
To make things look better we're led to believe
So much packaging, just for the display
You don't know what you have until you pay
Wrapped by machines running for twenty-four hours
Plastic looking people, selling plastic looking flowers
They ask 'Can we help? Do please call again'
Even my magazine has a plastic membrane
Ketchup bottle in plastic or glass
I have a choice at very long last
The main difference is the dreaded cost
I'm at my wits end and totally lost
At long last I'm at the baked beans
But they're sold in fours held by plastic rings
Even milk comes in different formats
A plastic bottle or a carton with flaps
My favourite butter comes in a plastic tray
So if it melts it won't run away
I reach the checkout, the queue is not funny
At least I can pay with plastic money
The checkout girl seems to be in a race
Pushing through my shopping at an alarming pace
Now I have to sign on the dotted line
I need my glasses to check it's all mine
That is when I feel real sick
Even my glasses are made of plastic.

Steven Cannings

A Coastal Walk

The shadows in the forest
They flicker across the path
Great trees stand upright
Old, tall and steadfast

The twisting path leads on
Sun glitters through the trees
Bright lights across the water
Reflects in what you see

Moving through the branches
One falls quickly to the ground
Suddenly the shadows gone
Without making a sound

Looking for unsuspecting prey
Geese gaggle on the shore
Spreading wings they swoop
Attacking fish diving for more

The rippling sound of the tide
Waves splashing on the shore
Lights sparkle on the water
Who could ask for more.

Elizabeth Hunter

NATURE

The miracle of nature,
Is so wonderful to see,
As it is shared with us each day,
For as we see nature's treasures,
I'm sure you'll agree,
They bring delight in every way.

Flowers on open meadows,
With swallows floating by,
Give delight in many different ways.
Daffodils of golden yellow,
Reaching for the sky,
Give the impression of warm summer days.

Bumble bees collecting pollen,
Busy floating by,
As they float upon the breeze.
Rabbits through fields go hopping,
With squirrels by their side,
Doing just exactly what they please.

On the pond, ducks are swimming,
Swans are also gliding too,
As upon the water they make their home.
Each day holds a new beginning,
A chance to see something new,
With every second glance you take.

Paul Secrett

MY FIRST AND ONLY LOVE

It was in school that we met
And he is someone I can't forget
He was my first and only love
His eyes shone like the stars above
His hair was the colour of the sun
Together we could have had such fun.

I'd see him when we'd change class
But he never smiled as we would pass
My heart would pound when I saw him
To me he really meant everything,
But he never took any notice of me
That made me sad but he did not see.

I'd see him at the school gates
I always made sure I was not late
I always missed him at the weekend
And longed for Monday to see him again,
I was too shy to speak to him
But hoped someday his heart I'd win.

I'd see him with all his mates
I guess they were talking about their dates
Oh how I wished he would have asked me
That would have filled my heart with glee,
Now thirty-five years on, I still think of him
Oh how I wish I could have worn his ring,
But I doubt he ever thinks of me
As I'm just someone he didn't see.

Eileen Kyte

AS THE BELLS RING

So long ago we said goodbye,
I shed a tear, heaved a sigh,
I would see you again
Often as I listened to a song,
Or looked at ageing photographs,
We would again be huddled in our den,
Or picnicking, playing cops and robbers.
Then came graduation day, so proud and proper,
Long black gown with satin trims,
A doctor now, you took your oath.
Then wedding bells and happy smiles
Before departing, flying free, far away
Many miles, to a country far from view,
Father died, people cried, the world not one we knew.
The days and years rolled on
As the tractor made its furrows
And the haystacks piled high,
The snow would come again and again,
White, then a slushy dirty mess
Before cleared by rain to a pristine cleanliness.
Mother died, again you came,
This boy in my dreams, greying now,
Reminding me of passing time
But memories are time capsules
Into which we may dip at will and wallow,
To my dear brother, health and a good year to follow.

Jacqueline D Rhodes

THE DOVECOTE

Stay warm and safe my sweetlings neath mother's feathered breast,
The sunlight makes you restless, but bide here in your nest.
Before you test your wings in flight,
You must learn the good from bad - the wrong from right.

Our home attracts so many birds and it is hard to know,
Who shares our corn on friendly terms, or who will be our foe.

The brightly coloured pheasant, his russet plumes displayed,
Will stay and browse the whole day through,
His constancy won't fade.
But you must beware the raven; black feathers hide the blackest heart.
He seeks the young and innocent, tearing tender flesh apart.
So listen well to what I say or you may come to rue the day.

The pair who come with seed and straw, you can depend on them,
Their pleasure is to see us fly, but their breed aren't all good men.
They'll wander round the garden as day turns into night,
And check that we are warm and fed, you'll see their friendly light.

The dove is still the sign of peace, but these are troubled days,
Yet in this peaceful garden, pray that peace will reign always!

Dorothy Brookes

THE TRUE ME

I do not want sympathy
Dressed in another motives garb
Or endless flowing words
That are just so much claptrap

I want no more - no less
Than those about me want
To be accepted for what I am
An not as some unholy mess

Oh yes!
The true me is somewhere
Inside this twisted frame
That stumbles and lurches
And some folk look at - and say
It's such a shame!

Johnny Someone looks and says
(Oh maybe not out aloud)
Poor thing; Oh it's such a shame
Looks at Mrs Mostpeople, and says
It would be kinder if . . .
Well! Still!
It can't happen to me.

Johnny Someone is really thinking
It would be nicer if they -
Weren't here for the likes of me to see

Johnny! Johnny! Don't you know?
That Jesus made the lame to walk
      And the blind to see

Johnny!
Such good news to tell - go talk,
Spread the good news
Through gospel word and song
Tell the despairing that there is hope
Tell the faithless that they are wrong
For Jesus can make the weakest strong
Come rejoice
        Rejoice in word and song.

Clive Cornwall

MESSAGE FROM HOLST

Venus plays,
Violin and cello sending shivers
Through my spine.
The melody haunts,
And turns my mind to a hilltop.
Sitting on a crag,
The memory fills my soul,
And I find myself gripping the chair arm
To calm the trembling hand.
My knuckles white,
My forehead moist,
My inside in turmoil,
Digestion disturbed.
Is it the Goddess herself,
Weaving thoughts with the waves
Of sound,
Lest we forget?

Anne Savan

THE HOMECOMING 1987

Ollie and Miaou, the tortoiseshell cat
Were both in the hall as I stepped on the mat
After flying from Cape Town without sleep or rest
Cramped in a seat behind a young pest
Who wriggled and struggled the whole flight through
Determined all sleep and rest to rue!
Completely exhausted and flopped in a chair
I came alive suddenly - away flew despair;
With one on my lap and one at my feet
My weary homecoming had been made complete;
An absentee for twenty years
Those family pets made me shed a few tears;
I said to my daughter and son-in-law,
'Now for sure I'm at home,
What could I wish more?'

'Tis later now by a year or two;
The morning's early and breakfast is through!
The play-room couch
Tempts me now to sit and slouch;
But Ollie's there up on the floor
And on my knee he puts his paw,
While appealing eyes gaze into mine
He knows the score - it is nearly nine
O'clock! We must slouch no more,
But get busy, like the bee.
Nature's beauty for to see,
Stretch our legs along the lane
'Twixt hedge and hedge, till the road we gain.
The Stoke Road hill, where the berries grow,
There are thousands there, row on row
For the birds to eat 'ere the snow arrives
Which both birds and Ollie homeward drives!

Claude A Knight

Who Is There?

It's quarter to three I should be asleep
I'm wide awake yet dare not peep
From under my quilt I've turned into a tent
I'm sitting upright with my knees all bent
The door is creaking there's a scratching sound
It climbed on my bed it's moving around
I put out my hand to put on the lamp
Something touched it, it was damp
Panic set in I let out a scream
Oh how I wish I was having a dream
But it isn't a dream this is for real
I can't explain how scared I feel
Holding my breath I have a feeling of dread
I dare not take the quilt off my head
I'm sweating now starting to bake
Oh thank goodness my husband's awake
He's pulling the quilt off my head
A furry ball leapt over my bed
'Kill it' I shrieked 'we've got a rat'
'Don't be stupid' he said 'it's only the cat'

Barbara Ramsay

ALONE WITH PRAYER

If you are depressed and lonely, too
There are things you can do;
Go to church just once, or twice, a week
God's blessings you can seek.
As you kneel and say a prayer
You will feel God's presence there.
When you get back home
You will feel God's presence *there*,
He *is* there and everywhere.
You will never feel alone each day
If you say a prayer each night and day,
God will lead the way.
When at night, you close your door
You will not be lonely anymore.

K Kay

ALONE

High in the heavens
      they passed me by
I heard their wild sweet cry.
A flight of geese
Southward bound
      across a greying sky.
I followed them
      with wistful eyes
Till lost beyond the purple hills.
I turned away and cried.
Last year we'd been together
Now I was alone
As I watched the summer die.

Ann P Tilt

THE DRIVING TEST

Put seat-belt on,
see that mirrors are checked,
if the make-up's OK,
then take the next step.
Turn key to start engine,
and with radio blaring,
wind down the window,
and check everyone's staring.
With the clutch fully down,
decide which gear to prepare,
release the handbrake,
and flick the hair.
Step on the gas,
and with the clutch up to bring,
find the biting point,
and start to sing.
Up into second,
and then into third,
get into fourth,
but mind the curb.
First on the left,
next on the right,
see gorgeous boy,
and flash the lights.
Reverse around the corner,
turn the car around,
and in true chick style,
cruise through town.

W O Z Warwick

MY RIVERSIDE WALK

I happily wander by the side of the river
strolling completely at ease
alone but not lonely.
Like a three-year-old in the confines of its garden
I delight in my latest new find . . .
the duck with her brood.
And like a three-year-old I watch in awe
as she pedals hurriedly, babies in tow, to a safe place
away from my wondering gaze.

Contemplating the mysteries of nature
I follow the gurgling river, wonderfully relaxed.
Like a young child without a care
I explore the riverbank . . .
amazed when I find a nest in the sand.
And like a young child I take a closer look
just to satisfy my curiosity and admire
the way the eggs are camouflaged.

The wind whistles around my body as I amble on.
In my quilted jacket and woolly hat
I'm protected from it snug and warm.
Like a child wrapped safely in its mother's arms
I feel free from all harm.
Its branches swaying the old oak tree stands reliably strong
and like a child leans against its mother
I lean against the tree taking shelter and strength from its stability.

Helen Crawford

ONE BROKEN HEART FOR SALE

We dated for what seemed ages, great memories, treasured moments
Now you're emigrating my life's taken a huge dent
How can you leave me behind and oh so all alone
But your mind's made up and soon you'll be long gone

Love you just can't walk away and leave me broken hearted
I've loved you from day one that our relationship started
People say that given time a broken heart will mend
I know where there's one for sale and I'll tell you where to send.

The big day has finally come and I can't face seeing you go
I should throw my arms around you, kiss you, but my heart's telling me no
Australia is a long way, but can our love survive the gap
You'll probably forget about me with so much more on tap

Now you've finally gone and walked right out of my life
You won't be coming back so I won't have to think twice
I'm staying on my own, no more women in my life
One more broken heart attack without using any knife

It's just a living existence drifting from day to day
A sad and lonely life I lead that's what many people say
Bitter salty tears are the only thing I taste
And photographs remind me of everything that went to waste.

Leigh Smart

JED THE FARMHAND AND HIS BROKEN HEART

My heart was broken, it had been ripped apart.
Now my pain came from an innocent start.
As the country blossomed in an early spring,
I was filled with a burning from within,
For a local lass from the village pub,
Oh that Sally and her wonderful grub.
Pie 'n' chips, ploughman's or shepherd's pie,
But 'tis not all, that caught my eye,
For that buxom Sally had such a smile,
It could melt a man to a quivering pile,
I was besotted, all my reason was gone,
But love being a funny thing, spurred me on,
So scrubbed and shinning in my only suit,
Fresh shaved, boots polished and looking real cute,
I headed for the pub and that special day,
Bound for true love and to give my heart away.
With a hand full of flowers picked from a green field,
I walked into the pub and before her I kneeled.
Suddenly there was silence, I felt my heart leap,
And there it was hanging for dear Sally to keep,
My pure and untouched truly loving heart,
She laughed grabbed it and ripped it apart,
'You silly young boy' she playfully said,
'To love you I'd have to be brain dead,'
The pub erupted in laughter and cheers,
And I ran for my life with an eyeful of tears,
Dear Sally had shattered my fondest dreams,
So for many days I planned horrible schemes,
To get even with her and repair the damage done,
But fate had not finished it was just having fun,
So it threw us together one dark stormy night,
And Sally found out that I was just right,

Now she is my wife and I love her a lot,
And so do the kids even the one in the cot,
Ah, but what of my heart all ripped and raw,
Well that repaired one stormy night in some dry straw.

Alex I Askaroff

Resolved

Yet again that time of year has once more come around
Where we all make rash promises, at least that's what I've found
We're stood together in a group, all stating what we think
While bursting out all over with excess of food and drink
And though we're somewhat worse for wear we know a cert solution
It's really easy-peasy mate just make a resolution
A few short words will put it right, it's easier than you think
To stop imbibing alcohol, you know the demon drink
Or giving up the ciggies, some spearmint you could chew
Though eating all that sugar could soon make two of you
In turn that leads to exercise, and lots of huff and puff
With running, pushing, lifting, till your body screams enough!
Maybe we'll try another tack, a diet's what's required
To leave you looking like Kate Moss? . . . You start like one inspired
But it isn't very long before the hunger pangs intrude
And you can't think of anything apart from that word food
Perhaps we'll tighten all our belts . . . Don't laugh it isn't funny
Living like a monk or nun just to save some money
So having thought out options, there's plenty there to choose
From saving all your money, to giving up the booze
You know what I've decided . . . Sorry to burst your bubble
I'm not doing anything, it's too much flaming trouble.

Brian Hemming

LOVE?

Confusion . . . a burst of adrenaline
Followed by the pull of anticipation . . .
Should this be heaven
Or the worst type of hell?
Constant struggle of
Instincts and desires
Between pride and insecurity
And dreams of happiness.
A whole new dimension
Where strong moods are governed
By the tiniest possible breeches of normality
Taken as implications.
Where other dreams are temporarily forgotten
In the hope of following
One stray desire
To a successful climax.
Desperation for another dose,
Another sniff of emotion
Stimulating continued existence
In the other world.

Aleksandra Tutus

BEAUTY IN BLEAKNESS

I love the autumn and winter seasons,
When nature's beauty is at its peak,
To see the year slowly die for God's reasons,
Look around and you'll see that it's not so bleak!

God sprinkles the snow on roof tops and people,
Lights up a rainbow after the rain,
The church bells ring within the towering steeple;
And children play in the snow driven lane.

Sunrise and the snow glistens like gold,
Enlightening the land and all within its reach,
The trees stand tall, bare and bold,
But it's the warmth that we beseech!

Out hearts are warmed as we look,
At cosy cottages with soft lights aglow,
By the side trickles a brook,
A cat paws the window, to catch the falling snow.

Outside a picket fence and stone wall,
That border most peoples abodes,
Are carpeted with velvet-like moss due to many a fall,
And moulds its character amidst country roads.

I thank God for the gift of sight,
And ask that I'd never take it for granted,
That He would bless those who live without light,
To see with their hearts, a vision pure and unslanted.

Dawn Madigan

A Child's Love

'Do you know what love is?'
My grandson said to me,
'Is it something that you touch,
or something that you see?'

'Can you smell it in the air,
or hear it passing by.
Can you taste it if it's there
and would it make me cry?'

'Why do you ask?' I said to him,
'You're far too young to know'
'But I want to' he said with a grin,
'So I'm prepared for it when I grow.'

'Well there's many kinds of love
but I can only explain a few.
Like the love we have for the Lord above,
And the love your Mum has for you.

There's love people have for their dogs
and the love children have for playing.
The love of a fire made from logs
and the love for a grandchild staying.

As for the love we all look for
well I'm sorry I can't explain.
When we find it, it makes us happy.
When it's lost it gives great pain.'

'Thank you Grandma,' the wee lad said,
'I think I know what you're saying
I love you Gran, here in my head
But I'd rather be out playing!'

Mo Lyon

A Silent Song

Love; love is the force of all life,
it opens up the thoughts from deep inside,
as daylight comes, it brings new thoughts,
with everyday and every dawn, love is the strength to welcome breath,
love is the gift to get the feelings out,
it's the force that can revive your life,
the power to wake you from your endless sleep.
Well I'm not sleeping anymore,
I can see the light of dawn,
I remember the tales of November, or was it December?
Monday, Tuesday, Wednesday, Thursday, any day,
sitting around with all the memories,
but I'm not sleeping any more,
the nightmares are real,
It's six am and I cry about the insanity,
but you're gone forever more, I won't see you at the break of dawn.
I dream about the times that were, what could have been,
but I'm not sleeping anymore, and this ain't a dream,
life goes on or so they say, but I've heard all this another day,
as time goes by life strays from the grey,
waking in the afternoons, smiling at the stainless frames,
goodnight I say, goodnight to all the memories.
Jesus Christ and God's delight are what will set the soul to flight,
I know that true love will never die,
one day I'll wake up in the morning when heaven's doors are gently yawning,
the true saviour the love creator will be there to greet me,
there will follow the greatest feast,
the endless feast of friends will begin with the dawn,
I will not be sleeping any longer.

__Brian Casson__

LOVE

Eros has twanged his bow
Young lovers wandering arms entwined
The soft touch, the gentle looks
The kiss which has no end
That wonderful world called love
The excitement and presents
the wedding dress in pearly silk
Lace flounces and flowing train
Wedding photography, cars and guests
Confetti, throwing a beautiful bouquet
Then away to a golden sunshine holiday
Yellow sands and brilliant blue sea
Time waits for no one.
The new baby in its mother's arms
Proud faces of family looking on
Grandma patiently knitting
This is love, everlasting love
the proud family, the new house
With shining paint-work and new furniture
A charming garden with flowers of every hue
The little pet woofing at the door
Bringing his lead, his faithful looks,
His eyes joyously asking, 'Take me for a walk.'
The wonderful new car
Its spaciousness, its colours
The thoughts of holidays to come
Its love of life and warmth and
All you can want to eternity.

Evelyn Ida Henfield

LOVE

Dear love, sweet instrument of joyous pain,
I fear that you strike me but yet again.
As mighty ambassador of my heart,
You unwittingly tear my soul apart
To burst within me and slowly subside;
You conquer my being, and there reside.
But lo, too often your name is applied
By those of ignorance, others who lied;
Your name used in vain, extorting a thought
Of a lesser sentiment - lesser import.
Love, ride amid the stronger emotion,
And stand alone with sister Devotion.
Remain, sweet instrument of joyous pain
And strike those others who've need of your gain.

Stanley W Croxtall

ABSENT FRIENDS

New Year's Eve for 1997
Thinking of friends on earth and in heaven
Days gone by when we were all together
Heedless of the winter weather
Enjoying ourselves and hoping forever
That our love and friendship would bind us together

Times have changed but my memory stays
And always will to the end of my days
Some friends are abroad or too far away
To spend the New Year with me but I say
Thanks for the memories and love that we share,
In thoughts you are present and I'll always care
Happy New Year to you all I say
and may God bless you on New Year's Day

Tess Whitlock

JANUARY STREAM

Lifeless stalks,
Rising starkly into the crisp, frost-laden air -
Brown stems of long-forgotten summer,
Erect in glacial water.
Willow tree, devoid of green,
Reluctantly trails its slender fingertips in the trickling flow,
Made sluggish by winter's rimy grip.

Now and then, a fragment of the frozen surface breaks free
And makes its stately way towards the sea,
Like a polar ice floe -
An Arctic Cleopatra in her queenly barge -
Only to be broken into myriad,
Diamond-like shards of ice,
As the stream (and ice) become a tide.

Victoria Schofield

NEW BIRTH OF SPRING

Pointing fingers to the sky
Anchors through the earth
Birds that sing a symphony
Spring that brings new birth

Silent now the mood appears
But surging through the arms
New life rushing, birds are gushing
Bringing love and charms

Ancient trees - how old are you?
What different lives you've seen
From the Lord and Master's house
Seeming dead - and then so green.

Mary Hulme

A Time For Every Season

Gazing from my window at a winter sunset,
Purples, crimsons, wonder never to forget,
I realised Mother Nature has her reasons,
Even for the cold, wet, darkest of seasons.

Children, espying snowflakes, faces aglow,
Rush outdoors to construct men of snow.
People, akin with Nature, know birds need
Help, providing bread, peanuts, wild seed.

We question, but Mother Nature knows best;
Her kingdom needs winter, the time to rest.
Deciduous trees sleep, stark branches bare,
Before reclothing for spring's fanfare.

Evergreens' hues stay throughout the year.
Animals grow thicker coats, so not to fear
Icy winds, whilst others have hibernated.
Less hardy birds, in late autumn migrated.

Long, dark evenings; humans stay indoors,
Resuming gentler pastimes, time to pause.
Soon, armies of snowdrops pushing through,
Are Mother Nature's signal; spring is due.

Slumbering animals stir for warmer times.
Birds return to mate, from foreign climes.
In the sunshine, people with renewed energy,
Join in natures sudden throng of activity.

Summer surely follows; the order of things,
Pursued by autumn breezes, birds' wanderings.
We cannot change Mother Nature's seasons,
Nor should we, knowing she has her reasons.

Janet Hewitt

NEW YEAR CELEBRATIONS OF A BABY ELEPHANT

It sways, it celebrates
The new year with us
It sits down as a child
At a party. It lets
Its trunk unfold and flow

Out like some fresh found toy.
Now its mother hoots and bellows
As the baby elephant
With ears flapping like leaves
And its trunk, a root,
Runs after the older fellows

And even when
It collapses into itself
It keeps
The power to enchant.

Andrew Baily

JESUS CHRIST

Justice was His sacred law,
Evil did He quell;
Simple was His mien and speech,
Utter was His spell -
So wise men tell.

Charity was His holy way,
He was peaceful as a dove;
Risen was His mortal flesh,
Immortal was His love.
Some say He's here to stay,
That Saviour from above!

David Stockdale

TRUE LOVE

Love can be found in many ways
And many different places
A true one will last you all your days
No matter what your life embraces
It will fill you with joy and gladness
On occasions when you are full of pride
It will comfort you in sadness
And bear you forward on life's tide
A mother's love is best of all
All her children she treats the same
She buffets them from every fall
And for any failure takes the blame
In youth the first romantic love
Is often pure and sweet
And if blessed from up above
Can mean your life's complete
The vows you make on marriage
Are a link not to be broken
They form the strongest carriage
For all promises then spoken
Love is a strong emotion
Which can melt the hardest heart
As deep as the deepest ocean
Are the feelings it will impart
So if true love should come to you
Then nurture it with care
Its warmth will always comfort you
And all life's pleasures you can share.

Doris Davis

A Pigeon's Nest

For the size of the bird
The nest is quite twee
just a hand full of twigs
in the arms of a tree,
no wonder the fledgling
made haste to the ground;
Fortunate next door pussy
was not around.
For a pigeon needs lessons
on how to build strong
so that the nest out lives storms
when they come along .
Mother is constant
and stays right to the end
but has little protection,
her eggs to defend.

The Painter in Words

Archie

He never questions my actions, or the things that I do,
    it's an unspoken bond, that we'll always be true
Together we play in the sunshine and walk in the rain,
    he's there in an instant, when I call out his name
He's been taught tricks, like for treats, give paw,
    and if I leave him too long, he pines at the door
He's a companion, a friend, a true best mate,
    even though last night, my slippers he ate
He's got deep brown eyes and a damp black nose
    and he's so endearing, that my love for him grows.

Lara Higgins

A Goodnight Kiss

Why are you so sad my child
When you're warm and safe and dry
Why are you so sad my child
When you're sweet as apple pie

Why are you so sad my child
So lonely and forsaken
Is it the lack of love you feel
I'm sure you're quite mistaken

So this is what you told me lord
When I was feeling sad and blue
And now I feel so guilty lord
Well I guess I never knew

You stood beside me always
Through every cut and slight
And as I lay me down to rest
You kissed a sweet goodnight.

Wayne & Christine Devlin

A Pint Of Dreams

The barmaid double pours my IQ brew.
I see lovers torrid in black velvet sheets.
A mountain range capped by snow and a swan diving into a swirling river of tar.

As the pint barely touches the sides, the lovers peak, the snow melts and the swan soars untainted into the sky.
The barmaid's voice breaks in, 'Would you like another?'
I said 'No you'll do!'

Kevin Turner

SNOWFLAKE

Winter morning crisp and bright
All around is frosty white.
Embroidered windows - near opaque -
Watch the dancing first snowflake.
That floats so gracefully to earth
Through frosty air that gave it birth.
The fragile form so crisp and light
Billows gently into sight,
Dancing on the north wind's breeze
Nestles in the arms of trees,
Thus created with perfection,
Guided by the wind's direction.
Floating, falling, graceful thing;
A feather shed from angel wing.
With its kin, on cold hard ground,
Breathes a silence quite profound,
That's as rent as children, cheeks aglow,
Tumble in the virgin snow!
Over country-side and town;
Spreads a shining eiderdown
To lend a warmth, that earth may bring
Awakening to the flowers of spring.
As the days grow dark and cold,
They note the year is growing old.
Then soon will fall a crystal flake
And a brilliant picture make.

Patricia Woodley

A New Year

The clock on the wall strikes midnight
As we raise our glasses in cheer
Auld Lang Syne is sung
The bells are rung
To welcome in the New Year

Many of us are sad the old year has ended
As it unfolds into the new
But greetings of good luck, health and prosperity
Are wished for me and you

It is a time for new beginnings
As we hope for our dreams to come true
A time for New Year's resolutions
I've made some, how about you?

If only there could be no more violence
A peaceful world for everyone
No more poverty, disease or killing
Let us make 1997 a good one

L A Brown

It's Like This

It's like when the day turns into the night,
or when loose clothing starts feeling tight.
It's like when there's less people in town that you know,
or when your memory loses it's get up and go.
It's when you can't eat anymore, and you've only just started.
Or when you see couples around, then find that they've parted.
It's like you're not quite as tall as you used to be,
and you try to focus your eyes, but you just cannot see.
It's like the films are now movies, they're just not the same,
is it the titles? Or is bad language to blame?
It's like you're male friends are not blokes any more,
they're guys now, and they all want to score!
It's like you can't sleep for tossing and turning,
and you've no more ambition, or yearning for learning.
I've wondered how I can measure my life span,
I'll tell you my thoughts as only I can.
It's like when you go for a fortnight away,
in my youth I'd just got there, for my short treasured stay.
At the end of the first week I'd got set in my ways,
Then when I pack to go home, I'm in my latter days.
It's like up to now I've still thrills to seek,
for I'm still on the Tuesday of my second week.
As another day dawns, I'm glad to say,
this looks vaguely familiar, like yesterday.
It's like day turned to night and darkness once fell,
now the sun shines so bright, at least for a spell.
I've life yet to live, and friends yet to meet,
if my weary body will keep up with my feet.
The days used to be when I was real nifty,
but, it's like this. . . today I've turned fifty.

Ronald Stanley Unsworth

THE LAST RESOLUTION

Towards the end of every year
A solemn, binding vow I take
To lay aside what I hold dear:
All pleasant pastimes to forsake.

It's not so hard to make the pact,
Then let those promises evolve,
But when, at last, I come to act
I'm often lacking in resolve.

Could it be because I'm weak
Or do I always aim too high?
A public image I must seek
This may be hard but how I'll try.

Perhaps this final pledge I'll take
Before I cease this yearly rite:
'New Year's compacts I forsake.'
There, now the future's looking bright.

Francis Marshall

WHERE AM I

When I look in the mirror
All that I can see
Is a person I don't recognise
Staring back at me

Locked away inside my head
Are the people who are me
Not someone putting on an act
For the whole world to see

Stephanie Waller

WHEELS

I'd had enough of bus queues and overcrowded trains
Plimsolls wet and soggy as I walked home in the rain
So I worked a lot of overtime, saved my hard earned bread
A car was too expensive so I bought a van instead.

It didn't run too well at first, the engine coughed and stalled
Till I had the brakes adjusted and the engine overhauled
I bought a rear view mirror, handbook and a jack
Stole my grandad's water bed and threw it in the back.

The paint work's bright and gleaming since I covered up the rust
The seats have sheepskin covers, the engine's free from dust
Lace curtains at the windows, Persian carpets on the floor
Mirrors on the ceiling, 'Don't disturb' signs on the doors.

Pulling girls is easy since I bought a Transit van
It turns them on to see me with my gear-stick in my hand
I impress them with the flash driving as I squeeze through narrow gaps
For my vision is restricted when they're sitting on my lap.

I drive through all the red lights, never wait till they turn green
Press my foot down on the pedals to make the tyres scream
I feel just like a film star as I drive around the town
Carving notches on the dashboard as I knock old grannies down.

I'm a pillar of society, I can hold my head up high
Policemen raise their helmets when they see me driving by
I'm the centre of attraction but I always play it cool
When people turn their heads round saying 'Blimey, what a tool.'

I love the sense of power as the engine starts to roar
When I bomb along the high street with my foot down to the floor
I'm mowing down pedestrians and before the blood congeals
I'm racing up the bypass, the proud owner of new wheels.

Maureen Lucas

LOVE

Enfolded in your arms so strong
Warmth, like a cloak wrapped round me
Tightly held against your heart
Love's gossamer thread has bound me
Your features etched upon my mind
Even when you're far away.
Your tenderness, your gentle touch
Stay with me each passing day.
At times I know the going's rough
Sometimes I hurt you deeply
But you forget so much so quick
Forgive me so completely.
Did I exist before you came,
Who was I without your name.
Love like a spring eternal flows,
Soothing, bubbling free
images locked within my heart,
to which you hold the key

Helga Morris

FIRST LOVE

I remember my first love, so besotted was I,
I would walk the long way home, just to get a glimpse of
the guy,
And if he walked past me, I'd have a sudden hot flush,
My legs would turn to jelly and my face would be a blush,
As my body seemed to boil and my face became red,
I would feel a strange pain, is it love? It's got to be
said,
And then one day to find he felt the same,
It felt like paradise on earth, hormones are to blame,
Being a teenager in love is a dangerous thing,
You give your all to dreams of an engagement ring,

After the first wonderful feeling comes the pain,
The heartache and disappointment and that strange feeling
again,
But eventually life goes on as normal, and you find
another love,
But one thing's for sure as time goes by you will never
forget that special first love!

Deborah Baker

WHAT IS LOVE?

What is love? Good heavens above . . .
Love is caring, love is sharing,
Love is like the turtle dove
Billing and cooing, willingly doing
Little things which show the love
One creature gives another.

What's love not? Well, quite a lot . . .
Not self-seeking, never speaking
Out of turn when one should not,
Never neglecting or resurrecting
From the past things best forgot
Which soon that love could smother.

Love of man for fellow man,
Self-effacing, always placing
Love atop life's complex plan,
Gently caressing, never distressing,
Clearly nothing plainer than
The love of child by mother.

True love never passes by,
So insistent and persistent,
Love nobody can deny,
Tugging the heartstrings at every parting,
No-one knows the reason why,
Lover, friend or brother.

Rex Taylor

You're All I'll Ever Need

Who is this whose glance is like the dawn?
So beautiful and bright.
As dazzling as the sun or moon.
A truly lovely sight.

Your hair is beautiful upon your cheeks.
It falls along your neck like jewels.
Such depth is your beauty, when looked upon,
Wise men, turn to love-struck fools.

Small and tender is your nose.
So soft your chin and cheeks.
Your lips, like scarlet ribbon
Are lovely as you speak.

Your delicate nick is round and smooth.
A striking tower of ivory.
As splendid as your chain of gold
With sparkling finery.

Your breasts are like gazelles
Twin deer stooped to feed.
Your scent more fragrant than the flowers,
You're all I'll ever need.

Your legs, the work of an artist's brush,
Like flames on melting candles.
How delightful is the curve of your thigh,
Just like your feet in sandals.

As breathtaking as a mountain range,
As pretty as a shining star.
Loveliest of women,
How beautiful you are.

Adam Griffiths

The Whispering Breeze

Whispered trails of glory
swamp my breast
touching the core of me,
clandestine thoughts
pick up the power
the river runs strong and true.

The singing trees
are there to bless
and caress
my deepening vows,
gently flows the breeze
the pain of love to ease.

For pain it is
it does not end with bliss,
for shadows fall
the world looms large
stands in the wings
leaves us on the brink of tears.

But all is not lost,
quiet recall
rekindling the warmth
like shimmering gold
in this blue haven
takes stock and grows,
to have and to hold.

Joan Hands

A New Leaf

As autumn's voice will order
Her loyal trees to unclothe
To obey every commandment the seasons have betrothed
Age will rake the olive branch
Scattering old leaves on the ground
Writing the old year's epilogue on every leaf that's found

The new year breathes a chivalry
Boasting a light upon the dawn
A knight with shining promises riding the brand new morn
The old year said its last goodbye
We salute its final tide
And memories sieved the memorabilia for the embarrassment and pride

Dreams simmered with a pretence
Chance offered a quaint bouquet
Doubt shuffled through the undergrowth to where optimism lay
Guilt protests its innocence
Habits ponder a question mark
Excuses blind our failures by hiding in the dark

Some moments lived in glory
Its importance bowed to thee
Some achievements are like a new-born child sitting smugly on the knee
Prospects were always welcome
Wherever the future roamed
This new year is another world bringing a prodigal hope back home

We inherited tomorrow
A new leaf in our dream
A fable of progression only prophets have ever seen
Yesterday pays its homage
Its resolutions are still pure
Thus the new leaf of our olive branch now hangs on the new year's door

David Bridgewater

Why-Why-Why?

When we are toddlers it's why, why, why
Whether we're outgoing or whether we're shy
Why, is a little word, but it means such a lot
Especially to me, being a little tot

Why Ma and Pa and all the other grownups
Can't answer my questions, when they start with why
They also ask, why, why, why,
But they get an answer, then why don't I?

I'm fobbed off with a 'because you can't
Go play with your toys or other little boys'
I doubt Ma and Pa know the answers
That's the truth, then they lose heart

Why, oh why can't grownups answer me
It would make my day, my mind would be free
Just one answer to my why's
Would make me feel I had won first prize

Olive Wright

Jabs

I don't mind injections
They're really not that bad!
And when it is all over
I must admit I'm sad!

I love all the equipment,
All kept clean on a tray.
And when it is all over
It's simply thrown away.

First they make your arm clean
By using a small swab
Of antiseptic something
Which does a lovely job!

Then they fix the needle
Onto a small syringe
And suck up this clear liquid
As you sit back and whinge!

Knocking all the air out
They say it will not hurt,
Of course, you've rolled your sleeve up
So you don't get blood on your shirt!

Then, before you know it,
The needle's in your arm!
It really is a struggle
To keep your cool and calm!

And that's all there is to it!
Except in special cases
When plasters are applied
And covered with smiley faces!

No, I don't mind injections
They really are quite fun!
But it's quite hard to sit down when
You've had one in your bum!

Gilda Ward

SHE CAME TO ME

How I cried so much in pain
I longed to see them once again
The Mum and Dad I used to know
I loved them both so long ago

It seemed forever they would be
Always here for you and me
As I woke in dead of night
A figure stood all in white

Gently speaking as I woke
Drifted away like a puff of smoke
Then I knew my prayers were heard
No one to believe it's too absurd

My heart felt peace at rest that night
The morning brought a brighter light
Always will I see her there
The lady in white I know who cares

Susan Goldsmith

AUTUMN

The shoulders of the hills stand bare,
Painted with wondrous colours rare;
From chalky white, iron red, to brown,
Streaked like a palette up and down;
While scarves of gold, and russet trees
In wooded valleys stand at ease;
And all about the brown and white
The hedges are ablaze and bright
With brilliant red of hips and haws.
Brambles dull are strung with gauze
Of cobwebs, thickened with wet dew,
Where rainbowed droplets shimmer through
The few dark berries hanging there;
And Traveller's Joy droops down like hair.
The meadows are new green again,
The year's fruition to attain.

Patricia Haynes

WHAT IT MEANS TO ME

Poetry means a whole world of dreams and fantasy.
When I say this I am not saying that poems are fantasy
but sometimes are about real life. Many people find
different ways of relaxing and ways to comfort themselves.
Some of my ways are writing, reading, and
listening to poetry. Anyone at all can write poetry
if they take it from the deepest depth of their soul,
heart and mind. I find the best way to express my
feelings are to write them in a poem. Many people
find poetry boring, but this is because they have not
found the right poem to suit their mind. To me poetry
will never be boring, it is a whole round of excitement.

L Futia

A Donkey's Day Out
(Matthew 20 : 1-11)

I was sitting alone eating grass one day
When I saw two people coming my way,
They stopped at my master and gestured at me,
Then came right on over and set me free.

But then they took me by my rope
And led me down a grassy slope,
To where a group of people stood,
And the looks of them were mostly good.

Me a donkey, a grey lot of fur,
Was then sat upon by a handsome sir,
The whole procession set off down the road
To where the sun on Jerusalem glowed.

Once in the city, we walked through the streets
Where crowds of people were beginning to meet,
Then out broke a cry of 'Hosanna the King'
And people around all joined in to sing.

They seemed to be cheering the one on my back,
Whilst to me it felt about to crack,
But still I plodded on through this place,
Trying to look filled with poise and grace.

The procession stopped at the temple door
Where the man on my back stepped down to the floor,
And then I seemed to be forgotten about,
Until a kind man came and led me out.

Charlotte Sainsbury

SPECIAL DAY

It seems so long ago
Since I told you that I love you so
I know you are so far away from me
Your letters, they bring such comfort to me
like an everlasting light that shines for me.
In this light I see you there, holding
out your hand
I make a move towards you and calling
out your name
But you weren't really there!
In my dreams we're together, touching and loving
forever,
But daylight comes, and I awake
just to find an empty space
The tears they fall, and I wipe them away
To keep them yet, for our special day.

T J M Walker

SOMEDAY

This is a time I'll never forget,
When you came to my house that day.
You told me you were moving
To a country far far away.

When it was time for you to go
We both began to cry
I'll never forget that moment
As it hurt when you said goodbye

I woke up the day after you had left
And in my bed I lay
I thought about you lots and lots
And hoped we'd meet again, someday.

Leanne Victoria Buck

GOD'S WORK - HIS WONDERS TO PERFORM

Just quite what happens I don't really know,
But it happened again last night.
I went to sleep feeling full of woe,
Now I've woken up all cheery and bright.
Fears for the future, no money for bills,
My daughter's boyfriend in trouble.
Headache, backache - all the usual ills,
Why does life have to puncture my bubble?
Yet now I'm positively planning my way,
Life's too good to feel down and dejected.
Rebecca phoned to say 'Have a nice day,'
The postman called - another poem accepted.
Although most of my life has been unmitigated mess,
    I've taken one good decision on board,
And now, while I sleep, my cares become less,
    I'm glad I gave myself up to the Lord.

Bruce Ward

FIDELITY

I can feel love in the air
A future for us both to share
I will use my own telepathy
You know it's an utter mystery

Our dreams will someday be true
You know our emotions follow through
I love your eyes that are mystified
Your feelings of me, you can never hide

We pray, for a lifetime of prosperity
With grace, refinement and fidelity.

Julian Matthews

PRICELESS TREASURE

Infatuated with each other,
O boy this can happen at
any age!
You find yourself engulfed
with feelings, you really
can't explain!

Bewitched with rapture
and they laugh at silly
things, only people who
have been in love, will
know what I mean!

You know how it can be
when they are apart,
that drives them crazy
with yearning, and the
emotional pain!

A moment of tenderness
O it can be so sweet!
A priceless treasure, that
only lovers hold dear
with cherished memories
for always to keep.

Esther Rehill

TREE HOUSE

And now it seems I've climbed a tree
to an empty blank space full of nothing
needs its fill of grace and loving
pulled into permanence the balance of owing
some heavy debt, not duty free

Now I'm retracted, full
of oyster-bed shells and
                     dropped
into a pit of feathers, where
nestling there I found a cross
giving grace to me through some sad loss
it says in the obituary

but it brought to life the hope in me
and I have planned my tree house for a church
where, in glad ascension through the leaves
visits me precious
but still unseen
a ghostly host

loving me
       down
so holy, and round me
filling this empty blank space
with nesting twigs of love and grace
hiding
from that searchlight face
behind the acorn leaves

Julie Ashpool

Assurance

I stand outside and listen to the church bells
Ringing in a brand New Year
I look into the future
And wonder what it has in store for me

I look forward to a starlit sky
And thank the Lord for this New Year
And ask Him for His guidance
All through the coming year

The Lord will honour His promise
The same today as yesterday and forever
No matter what we do or say
He will guide us through every day

I face the future without fear and
Wonder if I shall be here next year
So I am going to take life as it comes
And try to fulfil God's will for me

Sometimes the path I tread will be hard
So many things can happen in a day
But strength and courage will come my way
For Jesus Christ will always be my guide

We have nothing to fear as we go into another year
In trouble or strife joy or pleasure
All of which will come our way
Let's yield ourselves to God in prayer He is always there.

John Henry Bridgeman

The Feast Of The Turnover

Traders rub their hands with glee,
For little comes at Christmas free.
Though profits made will more than cover
The outlay on 'The Great Turnover'.
Some celebrants with ideas odd
Still sing of angels, birth and God,
While Wenceslas, The Bohemian king
With Hark The Herald Angels Sing,
Is put aside on Christmas Day
With other customs that don't pay.
Some churchmen still, with erudition,
Continuing long-held tradition,
Hope that trees and holly cast
A green veil on our pagan past.
And rarely church bells ring today;
It's not the twentieth century's way
For idle folk to homeward weave
Through crisping snow on Christmas Eve,
Where fairy lights with streets to cheer
And plastic Santas, year on year,
Adorn shops that they may entrap
More cash to fill the exchange gap:
Mammon and commerce rule all things
With little time for New Born Kings.
And at the end of tinsel trails,
Restaurant food and wines and ales,
With overflowing cash-draw till,
What was the season of goodwill
And peace on earth for every man
Is just another business plan.

Laurence Keen

THE SONG OF THE DOLPHINS

This is the song of the dolphins
As we speak with our squeaks to your hearts;
Let your forms with swift frolics take flight . . .
Do not think if it hurts, just try clicks of delight!

This is the song of the dolphins:
We did smile once so bright in deep past,
That our belovèd Lord, Jesus Christ,
Came down on a star to relieve the planet's strife.

This is the song of the dolphins . . .
Swim faster and breathe through the water;
Break seas inside you, heal all your waves,
May love move with grace in the pure bliss of your days.

Solomon Blue Waters

THE VILLAGE

Where are the meadows, where have they gone,
where is the grass that I played upon?
Where is the stream, where as a child I'd play for hours
imagination wild?
What happened to the footpath that I trod through tender years,
that led down to the village school, through trees that held no
fears?
Where has the village schoolhouse gone with its gate that
welcomed you there,
with the age-old graffiti *Billy loves Susie* carved with loving
care?
Where is the village shop that boasted general store?
Alas, with the heart of village life, I'm afraid it is no more.
Where once there lived a community thriving without fear,
Now there stands a *motorway*,
I'm entitled to shed a tear.

R S Hooper

THE GIFTS OF GOD

We thank You for the sunshine,
We thank You for the rain.
The one gives joy and gladness,
The other swells the grain.

The flowers and the bushes,
The blossom-laden trees,
The hands that tend the gardens,
We thank You, Lord, for these.

Some hands produce great paintings,
Some sculptures rare and fine,
While others make the furniture
On which we can recline.

You gave the minds that fashion
The symphonies we love,
The ballets and the operas,
The poems and hymns that move

Our hearts to praise and worship
To sing our psalms and laud
The One who made the heavens
And earth complete, unflawed.

The gifts of God are manifold,
We treasure every one.
He gave them out of love for us:
The best of all, His Son.

Joyce M Turner

BACK TO EDEN!

Birds have flown
from their nesty homes
to search for grubs
and dig for worms -
a lapse in winter
the snow has gone -
bringing hopes of spring
which won't be long.

A time for love
to recreate -
living things
all new and bright.

With hope we travel
along life's way
and patience keeps us company.
Faith in our Maker
Up above -
will teach us wisdom
will restore the love
The perfect love
between God and man -
bringing peace on earth
as our Maker planned.

Mary Skelton

MOUNTAINS

We tend to build up mountains
When we hit a little hill
And don't say that you haven't
For I know someday you will.
But when love comes your way again
And you feel your conscience bite
Just let your thinking guide you
And I know you'll be all right.

Now when you've hit a mountain
And your world has drifted by
Don't think of what you wanted
Or where and when and why,
But let your conscience guide you
Because it's nearly always right
It depends on how you argue
And why you want to fight.

Tony Jones

THE POOR OLD POLAR BEAR

He lies down
Bored and lonely
With nothing to do
Frustrated and useless
With no company
No friend to play with
He looks at the people
With sad unhappy eyes
Desperate to get out
To be free

Kerry Bennett

LOVE'S SAGA

It started with love,
And was spoiled by hate,
Not forever,
But during time.

Love restored,
Hate reviled,
Love forgave,
Hate forgot.

Love resurrected again,
Hate persecuted again.
Love persisted still,
And so did hate.
Love revived again.

Hate regressed again into bitter hatred.
But love continues into everlasting love.

Laurence Parfitt

MOVED AWAY

I moved away from
You now I miss you
More each day and night
We ring one another up and
Say how much we need
To be together and can't
Wait for the day we
Can hold one another in our
Arms and smile and say
We will never be apart
Or move away from our
Side till the day we die.

C Rodrigues

NEWNESS OF LIFE

Glistening, silvery paths
Like a smooth stretch of sand
Newly washed by the tide
Shimmering, saturated
Our future lays unknown
Step into the new moment
The untrodden, the fresh
Christ's spirit will mend you
Will comfort and tend you
If you believe that he lives now
Like wind whistling in from the sea
He will come to you
God, older than time
Younger than tomorrow
As a silver string
Silvery strands
Holding together

Jane Stagg

False Witness

When from the pulpit
Someone preaches a sermon
I sometimes wonder

Does he too believe
Or is he merely acting
Just playing a part

Who or what is he
That he dictates to people
And yet transgresses

Paying lip service
To what the church represents
We cannot be sure

There are sincere men
Who believe in what they preach
How may we know them?

Just one bad apple
Means that the rest are suspect
And we turn away

I will say my prayers
Daily in the privacy
And comfort of home.

John Carter-Dolman

FAITH

Events collapse around me,
Framing me inside.
A box of depression,
I close my eyes and imagine you here,
Shame that in a second I open those eyes,
To find you're not there.

This town.
Waiting,
Knowing,
A ghost town.
With the occasional spirit rising from the past,
Exclaiming, 'Let me entertain you.'

We dwell on thoughts.
With the morbid curiosity of a passer-by,
Who leaves the scene of a death.
We stare fascinated,
At the sadder state of ourselves,
When the darkness masks the bright inner light.

It's time for me to go away,
But I can't bear to take the bow.
Buy one more thing
That I don't really need.
I don't really need any more praise,
But I need faith.

We could all sink down low,
In a pool of perfectly maintained,
Self-pity.
Fortunately I have faith enough to know,
That despite my despair,
I will not fall as my Lord will be there.

Lee Ryder

The Heavenly Saviour

Everlasting in his heavenly presence
        Since man and woman were conceived.
Growing in hearts of those who believe
        Willing to listen to all who sinned
And forgive when shame is sincere,
        Thus vanquishing all guilt and fear.

He sent us His one and only Son
        To guide us in this old belief.
To cease the hatred that had begun
        And banish the burning lust and greed
Ending the evil that had taken hold -
        Allowing good to nurture from a loving seed.

Gone is the man who shone a sense of calm.
        Who cured the sick and helped the poor.
His love and forgiveness given to all.
        Cruelly crucified by sinners of the land
Their once warm and tender hearts -
        Hardened by the devil's hellish hand.

Stephanie Bones

YOU ARE WELCOME

Our church is warm and friendly,
It's a church that welcomes you.
At Christmas time it's glowing
With love and kindness, too.

Please, come in and join us
It says, please enter in
To join us singing carols,
Perhaps your favourite hymn.

We would be pleased to have you
For Christmas especially.
Even through the bright New Year
Please, bring the family.

See the tree that's sparkling
In church it gives us bliss.
We hope your hearts will warm to us.
We welcome you, God bless.

Jean Lloyd-Williams

In My Thoughts

Dear Betty, dear friend.
I want to tell you how much I miss you
And how I reminisce
About the times spent together
And love we had without a kiss.

I recall our first Holy Communion
On a bright November day
We wore long full white dresses
And danced and danced all day

I remember one September
We pinched some apples from a tree
We hid them in our knickers
And missed our bleedin' tea.

The many-a-said 'Hail Mary'
Kneeling on that shiny wooden floor
When I screamed out our fathers
I'd caught my foot inside the door.

And thinking about the orphanage
Outside Dublin by the sea
The nuns would take us walking for miles
We would end up bursting for a wee.

And as I reminisce
Thoughts of you still amaze
You made a beautiful Juliette
It was your favourite Shakespeare play.

I miss you dear friend
Still I go on and reminisce
About the times spent together
And the love we had without a kiss.

Kathleen Hurlow

AT WAR (THE BOMBING RAID)

They moan and shriek upon the horizon's edge,
Black skeletons of trees, clawing the mad gusts
Of plundering wind, spreading dawn's misery
Bloodshot across the window panes . . .

Oh, now to know I sleep!
With just one thought to wing to me asleep -
Clear out of time, to wake in that sweet, infant room,
Child-pale with young hours, edging the dawn
Gently astride old Berwyn Hills,
Soft-fingered clouds caress the brow of heaven,
And spill the hedgerows, blossom-littered o'er the
Hill, to flood the field deep fat in gold, along
Rock-chuckling Ceirog . . .

Sniffing death's stink in heaven's belly,
Gorge the dark brides of hate, bomb-bowelled,
Roaring for fragile man, monkeying his blood,
To twist God's image to a mocking thing.
Hellsmouth of sun, black crosses spewing, into
Our entrails, scream white heat, and fire decaying,
Mouth-boiling, blood-sweat prayers pathetic shine
Clear out, red, white and blue - help us, O God!
Help us! . . . Help us!

C Parry

WHAT'S PASSED IS PAST

Let's face it - friends we are but lovers not
We don't fit into that physical slot!
We touched in hope of past redemption
You know - that time we daren't mention!

Your priorities now are number one
Mine, self-respect - it has begun
You tainted a night by blatantly boasting
Defaced a secret smile with your mindless coasting

I trusted you with all I know
And now I awaken and choose to go
To think I even questioned uncertainty
Whilst you betrayed with dishonesty

All I asked for was trust and respect
Knowing past moments you don't then regret
Its category now - another lesson learnt
Rekindle old flames *and you get burnt!*

D Eales

BITTERNESS AT THE TERMINAL

With the hustle and bustle all around
Finding a quiet corner
Sipping from each other's lives
Between sips of coffee

Trying not to notice
Your cup tipping
More and more
Your head unconsciously tilting back
To drain the last drop
Already reaching out
For your coat and your bag

Making your dash for platform 3
My cup still half full
having to put another sugar in
Just to get it down.

Jenny Clarkson

PHONE BOX

He's not looking after himself
going pale and thin again.
Standing alone in a phone box
talking to me, listening to me.
It's raining outside,
that girl is naked in her bathroom again.
He's trying not to look, trying to listen.
I'm not there, the rain's not here.
We're lonely together on the phone.
They are laughing at me here, trying to listen,
To the boy in the phone box and the girl in the nude.

Vickie Simpson

SUSPENDED ANIMATION

I am locked in a vicious time-trap
And I know life goes on . . . but,
I've been left in the past, you see
I cannot move on, the door's been shut,
The memories that I shared with you
I just cannot leave behind,
Everyone tries to sympathise
And they all try to be so kind,
But I am stuck in this 'in-between'
And find that I cannot move on,
I am still back in 'that time and space'
Where I turned and found you gone,
So I will just remain back there
Until you return to me,
You must walk back into my life
So that you can set me free,
There is a good side, to all this
I will never more grow old,
The reason for this, being . . .
I have put my life on hold.

Deana Houghton

THE ROUTINE

He jumped out of bed
with fuel injection.

The turbo charged
race to the bathroom.

Pneumatic descent on stairs to
tight corner in advanced braking system.

Halogen on
for the toast smog.

The switch click and
slowly lowered window.

The power assistance in
close positioning to table.

The silent shift
to overdrive.

Chris Antcliff

SOUNDS

As I lie in my bed
My body settles down
I hear all the sounds,
that I did not hear before.
A hedgehog as it snuffles here and there.
Rattling the food on the plate it found.

Rustling leaves move gently in the breeze.
Scuttling in the rafters,
reminds me that the bats are about to fly.
The soft swish of an owl's wings
As it hunts prey through moonlight night.

A droning aeroplane passes overhead,
Going some place unknown to me.
What is that sound I hear?
Only water in the pipes cooling down.
I hear the sounds no more
As my mind begins to drift
To places far and wide.

Wendy Nobbs

Retiring In The Country

Christmas time has come and gone
But holly and ivy linger on.
They deck the hall, my living room
And chase away the wintry gloom.

I only walk a little way
To see another holly spray,
The ivy climbs on nearby wall
And seems to whisper 'peace to all'.

I live out in the country air
With green fields sprawling everywhere
Away from all the stress of town
I finally can settle down.

To listen to the birds in song
I've waited for my whole life long
The spring will not be far away,
I thank the Lord for each new day!

Joan Britton

Junkie

He hangs around the streets
Waiting for a pusher,
They finally meet in the dark dirty back street,
He has been taking drugs for about two years,
He knows he can't take much more,
He takes his fix,
His brain is in a mix,
He nauseates on the floor,
Well, this world won't be bothered with him anymore,
He's dead.

Vanessa Fitzgerald

LOVE

Your love is like a rose to me,
Growing stronger and closer to me,
Tonight you're safe,
Right here with me,
Right here in my arms,
Reliving through our memories,
Our hearts are beating with our love,
A love I feel grows stronger each night.

When you rise up and look at me,
There is no one I would rather see,
You make me feel so complete,
For our love is a rose,
Here in my rows of poetry.

I glow so bright with your love,
In a love I know will never cease,
For our love has risen into a certainty.
Leading us into eternity,
With love, warmth and so much more . . .

Sadie R Flather

Too Much

Too many magic mushrooms, too much LSD
Too many dabs of powder, too much Ecstasy
Too many trips on acid, too many tins of gas
Too much marijuana, too much smoking grass.

Too much crack cocaine, injecting heroin
Now your home is made of cardboard and your foodstore called a bin
Your blanket's called The Echo, your pillow's plimsoles caked in mud
Your friend is called Jack Daniels and you're used to spewing blood.

Breakfast's grubby chicken and a begged-for lukewarm cuppa
Then it's your daily treat - liquid lunch and supper
You haven't shaved for many moons or even washed your hair
You tread the city to keep warm, the children laugh or stare.

An invisible hand grasps your throat, another twists your chest
This will be your last trip, but probably your best
You want to shout, scream it out, but you smash down to the floor
Relief radiates from your smile, you're dead at thirty-four.

Gerard Phillips

Gulls

The cool, keen bracing Cornish breeze
That streams in gusts from off the grey-green ocean rollers,
Blows through my boyish hair.
And I, sprawling and supported by an elbow,
Am pink-faced and full of youthful zing!
Watching gulls in squawking, screaming squadrons
Circling and wheeling . . .
Before being taken by the wind . . . and then
Careering at breakneck speed inland,
They stop and turn;
And beating slowly up-wind, they rejoin
Their wind-tossed fellows, as in a dog-fight!

Edward Colson

SOMETHING FOR NOTHING

Bankruptcy stock to be sold off in lots,
Videos, radios, TV and hi-fi, books of all sorts non fiction to sci fi,
Furniture modern and furniture old,
Closing down sale the whole lot must be sold.

Second-hand autos come down to the auctions,
Give-away prices, driveaway bargains
Mercedes and Jaguar, Ford and Volkswagens,
Runners and bangers, the car someone lost,
Find them all here at a fractional cost.

Boot sale! Here today! Starting at six,
Empty your garages, empty your lofts, pack it all up and sell it all off,
Get a price on it now, large or small, old or new,
There's a dealer out there looking for you.

Down to the church hall for Saturday jumble,
Scanning the piles, searching for bric-a-brac, packing it in a sack,
Pennies to buy it! It's gone in a trice!
And it's off to the market at four times the price!

Draw numbers for you, everything free,
Immediate wealth, immediate prizes,
are they for real or merely disguises?
Take on approval, have it for days,
Forget to post it and then see who pays.

Invest in good companies, massive returns,
Finance agreement, interest free,
extending the overdraft, having a spree,
Purchase on credit card, take out a loan,
Your fortune awaits you, just pick up the phone.

Something for nothing? Buy your tickets fast!
Pick six from forty-nine, are they yours in a line?
Become a multi-millionaire with Lancelot and Guinevere?
Chances are, Monday comes, and we weren't even near.

Steve McIlroy

MIND-WARP FACTOR TEN

My head lay on the pillow, my mind was miles away.
My heart was beating soundly, as my thoughts began to play.

I saw a rainbow in the sky that changed to black then white.
And then my eyes glazed over, white orbs without their sight.

My body began to shiver, my mind began to scream.
The palms of my hands were sweaty - was reality becoming a dream?

Several arms began to push me, to the ground so hard and cold.
My senses wrenched from me - my sanity I could not hold.

Then a voice from above said, 'Kill him,' as I tried to scream a groan.
As I felt the fill of one last thrill of barbiturates and methadone.

And now my body lay empty of life and all its pain.
And now I look so peaceful although I died insane.

Chris Hails

JOE, STEPHANIE AND CHERÉE

This poem is for my children, Joe, Stephanie and Cherée
To tell them that I love them, they mean the world to me
I also thank the Lord He chose me from the millions
To bless me with the birth of my three darling children

Joe he is the eldest and my only son
I am really glad dear Lord that I became their Mum
Cherée she was my second, the first of my girls
The day that she was born brought joy into my world

Stephanie she's the youngest, the baby of the three
Each and every one of them is special unto me
I did not treat them different, I gave them all the same
The times that they were ill, I would have gladly took their pain

Each time that I was down and no-one seemed to care
I would glance around my home and always they were there
They gave me inspiration, a reason to go on
Our home is filled with memories from when each of them was born

I did the best I could and brought them up alone
We never knew what lay ahead, but had a happy home
We had our ups and downs like all families do
But the bond there was between us, always got us through

As the years have quickly passed, they're not babies anymore
Still I never go to sleep until they all come through the door
I worry all the time like all us mothers do
You will only realise when you are parents too

So you see my darling children, each special unto me
I would not change you for the world, you are my golden three

              God bless.

Donna Jamison

THE KA

Well, I leave the store and I see the crowd.
I smile to myself and I feel quite proud.
They're laughing and talking, their eyes aglow
As they walk around the star of the show
But the Ka is mine!

I'm driving fast up the motorway
When the bikers pass in disarray
Bowled over by the beauty of my dream machine
And the envy on their faces makes them green
But the Ka is mine!

She's the greatest supermodel in the land.
She's seen my Ka and you understand,
She wants to use it for the photoshoot,
The perfect accessory for the Westwood suit.
But the Ka is mine!

We're going racing at Newmarket
Take the Ka 'cos it's easy to park it.
The bookies wave and shout the score
While the punters love it and ask for more.
But the Ka is mine!

The horses stream out down the field
Who's to win and who's to yield?
There's a roar of welcome, cries of 'Fun!'
Clearly it *is* the Ka that's won.
And the Ka is mine!

It is a bold and dashing car, a really mean machine
That comes from the drawings of the Ford designer team.
It's a happy, sunny yellow Ka, elegant and sleek
And I'm the one who's sitting in the comfy driving seat
Because the Ka is mine!

Patricia M Sharp

THIEF OF TIME

Your dictionary, that thief of time,
    With words a shade bizarre
Like *zygote, spume* and *trunnion,*
    Pastiche and *samovar*

Diverts you from attempts to check,
    For spelling or for sense,
Some term potentially of use.
    It weakens your defence

To see so many pages scanned
    In tracking down your word
Resplendent with such gems as these.
    Bemused by the absurd,

You break off from your chosen task
    And, almost in a trance,
Allow the lexicography
    To lead you quite a dance.

Rewarded soon with *widdershins,*
    Galoot and *paradigm,*
You browse away contentedly,
    Forgetful of the time,

Till, suddenly brought down to earth,
    You hear the clock strike one.
Great Scott, you think, it's time for lunch.
    Where has the morning gone!

John Mallows

THE SCHOOL GOVERNOR
(Dedicated to Marsden CP School, Nelson)

The poor old school governor the person who gives all that time free,
There are about 16 school governors on a board,
But only about 4 or 5 care and do the work,
The rest just don't care a bit,
It's just a social status symbol to some,
75 per cent of LEA governors are a waste of time,
The teacher governors try but fail,
Because of the conflict with staff and others,
The head teacher has a right to be a governor,
The head teacher can't win at all any conflict,
Any complaint the head teacher always takes the fire
It is hard for teachers to keep up with new skills.
When there is no money for training,
No money for children's books some date back to 1960,
In fact schools need more cash,
After over 17 years of Tories who say they care,
What will the year 2000 bring us,
Will the schools and the NHS go down the drain?
So what's to come the future looks bleak,
Your school's just fallen into bits,
And when an old school governor looks back,
At the hours of free time he or she has put in,
Will they think it's been a waste of time spent,
After all no-one gives them any thanks,
But a good school governor plods on till when,
He or she becomes old or ill and gives up,
No one ever says 'Thank you, you cared,'
But you still may have time,
But it's too late for some,
They are now in the grave God bless them,
But at that old governors' rest home,
Just over the hill you still have time to say one 'Thank you.'

Donald Jay

THE DEAR GARDEN

I lay in the garden,
Where the tall willows weep.
In the flower field next to it,
Graze healthy, fat sheep.

Slowly I arose from,
my patch on the lawn.
I glanced to the trees,
And there stood a small fawn.

Its large brown eyes
Did seem to say
Please follow me,
Do come this way.

Then he bounded,
out of my sight.
So I ran after him,
Nearly followed all night.

But then I found,
that was not to be.
The young deer,
Stopped, just ahead of me.

And when I looked,
I did find.
A secret garden
with a world of some kind.

Where the fairies dance,
And the elves did play.
A great sense of happiness,
filled me that day.

Then suddenly, bang!
It started to rain.
And I'm lying in
My garden again

Was it a dream?
Or did I really go?
I suppose that is something,
I never shall know.

Katherine Smart (12)

KATY

Katy is a lovely person,
Full of energy and life
She puts many of us to shame
When she decides to use
Her motorised wheelchair.
She presses buttons,
These she knows make it go,
Be it forward or back,
In and out of narrow corners
What a clever lass!
Just see her cope
With all the obstacles
Fate has put in her way.
Makes me wonder, why I grumble
My problems are non-existent
Compared to Katy's.
Her family are a tower of strength
To this little girl
We are all so very useless
Compared to Katy.
You see she has cerebral palsy.

Linda J Proom

Dare To Dream

Dare to dream and strive to be
The person that you wish to be
For wishes come true every day
For people who believe they may

Reach out your hand and touch the stars
They're within reach, don't stop, don't pause
To think that it will all turn flat
Let lesser folk worry about that

Your life is paved, a steady road
Lies arrow straight in front of you
And at the end a lighter load
If you believe it can come true

That path is laid with slabs of hope
By family and friends met on the way
Keep dreaming on and you can cope
With all that life can throw your way

Norman Wright

8 Hours a Day

Here we go again
Monday morning
it's the start of more pain
I sit in here and think to
myself deep thoughts
that are only ever for you.

Here we go, here we go again
8 long hours today
you know it's a constant pain
I only want to be with you
for this is killing me
and I pray it will soon be through.

8 hours a day
stuck in this place
8 hours a day
paid slavery, you could say
8 hours a day
in this awful place
8 hours a day
it's such a disgrace
8 hours a day
with thoughts solely for you
8 hours a day
God knows
I miss you.

P J Gassner

COMING TO THE END OF LIFE'S JOURNEY

My time now here is at an end,
No one to turn to, not even a friend,
All gone before me except the young,
All with their own lives, too busy to see
Just how lonely life has been,
These past years.

A call now and then, helped a lot
Even though they care,
They've little time to spare,
To help ease the pain of aching heart and limbs.

The body has got so frail,
Someone comes in to help wash and dress.
But when they have gone, and the day slips by,
With thoughts going round in your head,
Remembering all that you meant to do,
Plus all the things you meant to say.
What does it all add up to?
But then, I guess it's just the same
For everyone else at life's end.

P Wright

THE OLD ANTIQUE DEALER, MY FRIEND

He's gone
My loss overwhelms me.

In the chapel
Some grieved, some grasped.
And, as the priest didn't know him
He talked about religion.

I was glad to escape.
I drove for miles
Along the winding lanes of Lleyn,
While through my tears the winter sun
Shone upon its fields and hedgerows.

Proud, rough, canny 'Duke',
Ancient sage, nature man.
That is where you were that day
Earth to earth
And living on.

Leila Maryat

ODE TO ALANNA

Alanna, you're a little treasure
You give us all so much pleasure
The day you came home to your Granda and Grannie's
We all stood round like excited nannies

We had waited and waited with excitement and wonder
But as soon as we saw you our hearts fell asunder
We'd been told how beautiful you were, in fact
But we weren't prepared for quite such an impact

On that first day we made such a fuss
Because you were so special to us
Your cousins were there to greet you as well
And you've given us all lovely stories to tell

But if you think that we were glad
That's no comparison to your Mum and Dad
Your Mammy carried you in through the door
And your Daddy filmed that and much more

We know when you're all grown up and wise
That you'll surely come to realise
Why we think of your Mum with such high regard
And glad our beloved brother is your special Dad

They're a wonderful couple who really care
And they've so much goodness they want to share
They are so big-hearted and genuine too
They want to divide their special love with you

Don't think we're prejudiced because of the name
'Cos anyone who knows them will tell you the same
Now their ultimate dream has come true
And this was made possible; all thanks to you

However, they know this poem is not about them
It is all about you; you little gem
So we'll end with the unanimous family slogan
'Welcome; we all love you Alanna Rogan'

Magdalene McKinney

HURT

The hurt inside me, is Oh so bad
I really can't tell you how much
The reason why, is Oh so sad
My heart feels it's had an almighty crush.

Please excuse the water in my eyes
But, this is what we call pain
The light within has withered and died
I really am fighting deep inside.

Each day, I know will get better
Even though I feel there's no end
And nothing in this world matters
Thank God for all my friends.

They have kept me going each day
Just by being there, close by.
I really do try to listen to what they say
I'm fine, I try to say, but they know, it's a lie.

J M Lerigo

THE FLYING VET
(Dedicated to a friend who gave up a brilliant veterinary career to minister to the needs of the people in Papua New Guinea)

You said you'd do it, and you did
You gave up all so they might live.

Day by day you learnt to fly
And notched up hours in the sky;
Across the seas you then were sent
To learn new skills was your intent.

My friend I may not understand
How each day now you fly the land
Creeping through holes of cloud and rain
To land on slippery mount'nous terrain.

How can you be sure my friend
There'll be an airstrip at the end?
Nor what welcome you may get,
They may need a doctor, nurse or vet!

And though I miss you I confess
You mean the world to them I guess.

Hilary J Hulford

KARAOKE QUEEN (NOT)

I should have known better at my age;
I've never had much of a voice,
But everyone else was having a go
So I really had little choice.
Besides, I'd had a few whiskies,
And felt as *relaxed as a newt*,
So I eagerly took hold of the microphone,
To show off my fine attribute.
I sang a rendition of 'Crazy',
And that's what I must have been
To let myself be persuaded
To go near that wretched machine.
But that's not the end of the story:
Someone, whom I thought was my friend,
Had video-ed the entire proceedings,
Ensuring I couldn't pretend
I'd given a sparkling performance,
And sounded just like Patsy Cline,
Still, I'm brilliant at belting out 'Simply the Best',
So I'll be Tina Turner next time.

Delia Bennett

IN MY THOUGHTS

It must be years since we were in the school choir -
Then we moved from first year to higher.
I heard your Mum and Dad had died - so did mine -
remember them?
I miss them so - how much they will never know.

We must be missed in Howfen town the place we both were born -
It is more than forty years ago since we lived next door.
Remember the church walking days, and your awkward ways?
I was jealous when you were Rose Queen -
You were more confident than I had been.

Eventually you got your man - you left the town at 21!
You were always the ambitious one -
And married a young Australian - I'm sure you made him a good wife
After forty years you must have enjoyed your life
In the backwoods sheep farming somewhere.

I have not seen you since but visited Howfen town
saw your sister who gave me the news -
So to you I must write this very night -
Once we were so near now so far - the other side of the world -
And yet I think of you.

M E Smith

NO TIME TO STOP

No time to stop
No time to think
I live my life right
On the brink.

I see the signs
I take no care
No time to stop
So snails beware.

The red light, to me,
Does not exist,
Life is my speed and
Speeds my wizz.

The traffic, you'll see,
I'll pass by,
I live for speed
No wonder why.

Amii Rowlinson

MACHINE AND MAN

Engines roar, the start of the race
Into the first bend, setting the pace
Opening to full throttle on the straight
Manoeuvring the machine with masterly grace

Machine and man leading after several laps
Rival opponents edging through the gaps
Twisting and turning and speed turned full on
David Coulthard, racing driver, Formula One
Past the chequered flag, he has become
A well deserved titled European champion.

Rita Humphrey

GROAN AND MUMBLE

Let's have a moan and grumble,
Let's have a worry day.
Let's put aside one dozen hours
With nothing good to say.
Let's begin at 9 am
A Monday would be best,
We'll carry on all through the day
Without a single rest.

We'll moan about the buses,
The weather, and the food.
The neighbours, and the neighbour's cat,
Their children are so rude!
Their noisy radios that blare,
And blast our tender ears,
How can they show such disregard
Of our advancing years?

What a state the house is in
We'll never get it straight,
The garden needs attention,
And the latch is off the gate.
The pot plants look a sickly crew,
I don't know what they're needing,
I'm sure I've done my best for them,
Perhaps they just need feeding?

The milkman hasn't called as yet,
So he will have to go!
I s'pose he'll have a good excuse,
He'll blame it on the snow.
Oh dear! Oh dear! I've got a pain,
Is this another hurdle?
Or does it mean I'll have to slim,
Or loosen up my girdle?

An awful thought has just occurred,
I'm starting to feel fine,
I've finished all my grumbling,
And it's only half past nine!

Joyce Mason

FOREVER FRIENDS

Christine is my absent friend who lives so far away
I must admit I think of her at least once every day
She used to live next door to me but I returned across the sea
Back to England, to my home, now we only speak by phone
Our letters few and far between,
Although family videos sometimes are seen
When we talk we both reminisce
Of all the things that we did and we miss
The keep fit and exercise on my kitchen floor
The swimming and shopping and so very much more
Although New Zealand is so far away
We have to believe that there will come a day
We'll meet up again and have more good fun
And catch up on all the things that we've done
One thing that's happened in our years apart
Our kids have grown up and they've made a start
At making us grandmothers, so we've lots to compare
There's photos to swap and stories to share
The world's getting smaller we often are told
But fares are no cheaper and I'm getting old
I know this won't stop me, there will come a day
I'll see my friend Christine there must be a way

Sandra Pocock

LIFE ON THE STREET

He'll be down in the park, looking tired and stark,
Unshaven, unkept and unwell.
A bottle of meths in a plastic bag,
Living in a lonely hell.
Once a proud man with a dream and a plan,
A job, a home and a wife,
Now he's looking for digs, and never forgives
A system that shattered his life.

Further on in the park, just after dark,
A bunch of half drunken kids.
No more than thirteen and they've already been
To the pushers, the pimps and the skids.
They'll throw up on the bench, collapse in the stench,
When no weed and no cider remain,
Wake up, find a joint, get stoned to the point
Where they're floating, they feel good again.

Bellied up to a bar (they are all on a par)
Any town you may happen to be.
Someone will appear in the mist of the beer
Offering uppers, downers, or 'E'.
While out on the street, using their feet
Kicking some poor kid to bits,
They're out of their mind and totally blind
From the booze, the drugs and the glitz.

To the girls gathered round, they're the heroes they've found,
In some bar-room, or night-club, or rave.
And who cares a toss, it isn't their loss
If the victim ends up in a grave.
And a good time whatever the price
It's the way they must go, and they don't want to know.
They live in a fool's paradise.

It's not wise nor nice to give them advice,
Indeed, it's a sign of the time.
They can't see a future where there isn't a hope
It's the system sir, causing the crime.

It's life on the street, and the young are forfeit,
But that's what they've chosen to be,
And none are so blind, as the do-gooding kind
And a public who don't want to see.

Ernest Hall

THE MORNING AFTER THE NIGHT BEFORE

I've drunk the dirty midnight oil
eyes leaden, glazed and weak.
Pen poised like heavy musketry
to pepper the empty sheet.

Thoughts blasted my brain like bullets
richocheted around my head,
in fast decreasing circles
imagination's dead.

Crumpled pages lie around me,
distorted, cast away.
So many words are wasted,
there's nothing left to say.

Lee Silvera

You

When my life has come to its closing
When the sunshine's warmth fades away
When the breath of life within me
Is finally ebbing away
Then the memory of the landmarks
That made the journey worthwhile
The mountains climbed, the dreams fulfilled
May bring to my lips a faint smile
The tender arms of children
With their innocence and joy
Will sparkle, each a jewel
So precious, girl or boy
The friends who gave me comfort
When the road was long and hard
With confidence sustaining
When my soul with pain was scarred
So many happy times gone by
Will flash across my mind
But in a corner stood alone
A special thought I'll find
A thought of you I'll set aside
With love I'll say goodbye
And gently set your memory free
But not until I die
For here within my heart you'll live
Until my life is through
Of all the beauty life did give
Of course this thought of you
Will be among the treasures
That I hold so dear and strong
And you'll be here deep within me
Like the echo of a song

Pauline Bell

STARGAZERS

On a vivacious sand dune
The month was hot summer June,
A holiday season
In western world's calendar
Pale smile of a crescent moon.

Time was night
Dark, deep, serene calmness
By the Atlantic.
They sat side by side.
Gazing at the sky, he said
'Hi! It is definitely *Proxima Sentorai.*'
She shook her head, then said
'No - no my dear
It is the *great polar star.*'
The crescent moon
The dazzling stars, cool breeze,
Sea touching quiet pier
For no apparent reason
They began to whisper.
They came close, held hands
Then uttered sweetly
In a French Riviera, a French word
'Mon ami.'
The blue Atlantic flows heedlessly.

Different destinations next morning
A tune sent forth from a pretty violin.
Ages after, says the girl
I remember you
And also blue Danube.

Saleha Chowdhury

INSEPARABLE

A Tribute to Ladybirds

A ladybird, that had spent the winter
Asleep beneath a splinter,
Lands upon the roses
Like a cartoon hand-grenade
That a camera superimposes.
Another, that instinct had laid
In the luxurious bark of a pine,
Is as dark as a spent land mine.

*The New Forest Badger Watch, Burley:
Exposed*

Some badgers, adjacent to the hide,
Stared and modified their paces
As if the glass had magnified,
Fleetingly, our feet and faces
And we were visible in the night,
Beneath a lens and whiplashed light.
My pulse and paranoia concurred,
Perhaps my tinnitus could be heard.

These words were warmed by the mittens of tears,
When they were written in Hordle
For Hordle, a pigeon who was very brave,
Who we hoped the surgeon of prayer would save.
We are, all three of us, friends,
Beyond where awareness ends . . .

Rogan Whitenails

GULF CONFLICT

The conflict that rages in the Middle East,
Will be the subject for many to write,
It may be easier for me at least,
Because here it is so, so quiet.
I'm following with interest, being first of the few,
The plight of our lads far away,
Good God, if some of them only knew,
That to come, was their longest day.
'Tis a repeat of war days, long past,
When the world gathered together its might,
knowing full well the die was cast,
Through darkness, they sought the light.
No one but no one ever expected a repeat,
There was no way a war could start,
I tell you truly there is no defeat,
A message straight from my heart.
Let us all in unison, express our thanks,
To the boys in the air and the lads at sea,
To the soldiers in their tanks,
There's never been a war like this, you see,
Three cheers also for the Yanks.
With all this terrible bombing,
With everything covered in sand,
For home they are all longing,
To return to this dear land.
From John O'Groats to Birmingham,
We hope they will answer the call,
To put to flight this guy Saddam,
And return home ten feet tall.
'A Long Way To Tipperary' was a good old song,
Remembered and sung by the bold,
Our sons now sing as they march along,
Their story one day to be told.

J W McCarthy

IN MY THOUGHTS

Oh Dennis it's just memories now your Labrador's so old. Fifteen in doggie years, he can no longer stand the cold, or walk up steps untiringly, then race you to meet me, with waggy tail and golden coat, what a joy it used to be.

In wind and rain by the downs and sea, how he loved the beach and swam back to me. All the photos I took and the picnics we had. Yes Trigger you loved them as much as your Dad.

I am glad you came from London to see this place so rare. The scented flowers, the singing birds, the fresh and pure air. The sunsets in the evening and the sunrise in the morn. No sight could be more beautiful to a camper on the lawn.

With your dog in bed and you on wet grass, you awoke to a navy blue sky and the moon and the stars. In the long summer days we chatted for hours, while Trigger ate pies and smelled the flowers.

When you and Trigger left me last, his eyes were full of tears. I wondered why, but now I know he was so old, he had to go so very soon to heaven. Now we are sad, but one day we will meet and then once more he will play around our feet.

Julie Holmes

LIFE IN THE FAST LANE

Life in the fast lane
- a constant drain on energies
A chain of 'megastars' and 'movie queens',
'would-be's' and 'has-beens'
False hopes, shattered dreams.
Business brunches,
Champagne lunches,
Making a deal -
It's a steal for the agent,
Ever diligent, he'll pick up the bill and
Swallow a pill for his stress . . .
His hair's in a mess as he
runs nervous fingers through strands of grey,
It's the same line each day - so
Why does he stay?

For money, the power and the glory.
One day he'll write his story
of their capers - and sell it to the
Sunday papers.

Then *he'll* be 'someone'.
He'll be known.
The Press will be on the phone, hounding,
pounding on his door
Looking for their pitch . . .

Then - back in the fast lane!
Life's a bitch.

Gwyneth M Glascodine

THE ILLICIT DRAM

In days of old when men were bold,
Many stories have been told,
Of Revenue Officers trying to follow
Smugglers to the hidden hollows,
Where a cooking worm and a single still,
Produced the illicit dram of the hills.

In Highland areas, nearly every farm
Had a still. They raised the alarm,
When Excise men were seen nearby,
They hoisted sheets or flags on high,
To warn the others their utensils to hide,
Before the men were by their side.

On one occasion at an inn,
Excise men thought they'd had a win.
In an upstairs room they guarded the whisky,
They didn't think it was very risky.
During the night the kegs were spiled,
As the whisky drained, the smugglers smiled.

The smugglers moved their contraband
By various means over sea and land.
Women receiving fond caresses,
Hid whisky under voluminous dresses.
Preachers preaching of the missing lamb,
Under the pulpit was the illicit dram.

Cartloads of whisky defended by men
With pistols and bludgeons they travelled the glens.
With Excise men they had pitched battles,
They didn't have time for idle prattle.
What they did they knew was risky,
But they did it all for a dram of whisky.

Janet Boulton

THE REFUGE

Why is it always in winter
That the heating decides it will quit?
Why does it do it when I'm below par,
And not when I'm healthy and fit?
Then, when I'm getting better
Does the noise of the workmen begin,
The sawing, banging and hammering
Causing no end of a din.
I sit here miserable and shivering,
Feeling down-hearted and blue,
They say they'll be finished tomorrow
Oh, how I hope that is true.
Meanwhile my spouse, ever thoughtful
Says 'Let us adjourn to the pub,
Where it's friendly and warm and cosy
And they're serving real ale and good grub.'
No sooner said and we're down there
By the fire with a glass in our hand.
As we eat and converse with a genial mine host
We relax and the feeling is grand.
One glass leads to another
I am drowsy, the evening's just sped,
I suppose it is time that we sallied forth
To that, Oh so cold house and our bed.
If the work isn't finished as stated
It really won't cause me much sorrow.
We've had such a good time this evening
We'll gladly repeat it tomorrow.

Nellie Heard

THE MORNING AFTER

In downtown Hollywood, film capital of the world, it's 4.59 am
the morning after the glittering 'Oscars' ceremony,
an unknown actor is now the toast of Tinseltown
awarded for a performance - the finest of any actor in living memory.
A battered wife gazes into her mirror as she scrutinises the physical
scars and soothes the destructive self-image that have resulted from
'25 years of wedded bliss'.
It's the morning after she has discarded her tyrannical brutish husband
Oh! How she has never experienced joy such as this.
But an idyllic English country town is stunned and shocked
by the night-time discovery of another blood-splattered body
lacerated from head to toe.
On the morning after the local constabulary have been outwitted
by this psychotic serial killer yet again
as their investigation has been dealt another cruel blow.
A cataclysmic race-riot tears apart the nation,
all citizens link arms in unity the morning after
to restore the country's pride in deliberation.
The armed forces, the police and the fire service are greatly revered
as they reconstruct the charred remnants emanating from this
explosive act of hate.
All politicians cast aside differences the morning after to ponder
over this country's fate.
Big Ben chimes at 12 am, January 1st,
to herald the beginning of a new year,
It's the early hours of New Year's Day the morning after
New Year's Eve, the ultimate climax in festive cheer.
Amid the half-hearted resolutions, alcoholic hangovers,
celebratory music and shrill sounds of seasonal laughter,
blank faces gaze aimlessly into space at the prospects for the future
on this particular morning after.
And as I reach out the morning after last's passionate
embrace with my lover,
I'm desolate and distraught by his hastily scribbled note that he's
left me for another.

But today is like any normal day as I prepare to return
to the corporate world of employment a most unwelcome return
though with another failed attempt at love to undermine me
this morning. Oh! Will I never ever learn?

Finé Buliciri

AFTER ALL THE MONTHS

After all the months
        of longing, with my head
In the clouds, last night
        you came into my bed.
Common sense, if I
        had any, would say,
That it should not have
        happened: but today,
The pillow is still warm,
        where you lay your head,
Before you rose and dressed
        and oh so softly said,
'Au revoir' (I knew
        that it meant 'goodbye')
Lying here, I'm trying
        so hard not to cry;
And living once again
        each precious kiss, each touch,
Each tender word you spoke;
        and loving you so much.

Patricia Cook

I Wake Alone

I wake alone, I always wake alone.
On the side a crumpled phone number and a champagne cork,
trophies of a Saturday night.
I won't phone, I never phone.
This one was young, oh so young,
full of life and passion.
An unwitting player in my games of lust.
Tomorrow I'll be gone,
new assignment, new town.
I'm a free spirit, a nineties woman,
I don't want a wedding ring.
But I have needs, sexual needs,
I'll find someone, I always do.
But I'll wake alone, I always wake alone.
And I won't phone, it's my only rule,
I never phone.

Karen Hutton

For David Holbrook

I remember you, on the first occasion we met,
Crossing Midsummer Common from the Fort St George,
Where we had sat to leaf through the submissions
Made to a writing competition.
                        You carried a stick
As your books were carried, when I began to teach,
Like the field marshall's baton
By every trooper in the ranks
Of the sensitivity squad.

I would like to meet you again
Now that I have discovered,
What you have always known,
That there are more important things in life than poetry.

Stan Downing

Times Past

Strolling through brittle leaves
Carpets of gold so vast,
Warm thoughts of someone dear
Remembering times past.

Thinking of the happy days
And those of sadness too,
From little girls to teens
A precious friend was you.

One who always listened
To secrets that I shared,
Through laughter and the tears
You were the one that cared.

Failures and successes
Sometimes a heavy load,
Tenderness and caring
To help me down the road.

Bridesmaid at my wedding
Godmother to my son,
We travelled through life's way
Before our day was done.

Then came the rainbow's end
As you went far away,
To happiness anew
Before dark hair turned grey.

It's time now to stroll on
But you are with me too,
In that piece of my heart
That just belongs to you.

Helen Kemp

DEDICATED TO MY FRIEND

How beautiful the flower of friendship,
The bond between us we hold dear
And the tie that binds, grows stronger
As our friendship stands the test of years,
Dear friend when'er the path of life grew rough,
You offered me warm sympathy,
A listening ear to show you cared,
A better friend you could not be
And now that you have sadly moved away,
I miss you more than words can say,
I miss the tête-à-tête with cups of tea,
Few others have your genial personality,
We've weathered all the storms of life together
And we've shared the blessings of fair weather,
The happy days spent travelling,
Fond memories to treasure
And the quiet hours at home, relaxing at our leisure,
In your new life, with all my heart I wish you well,
Our friendship will not end, it has yet more to tell,
We'll keep in touch and have long converse
on the telephone,
When I'm around you'll never feel alone,
I'll come as often as I can to stay with you,
We still have much to look forward to,
Thank you just for being there for me
Throughout the changing seasons, loyal, true,
I hope that I have ever been as good a friend to you.

Marjorie Doris Walshe

WHAT'S A FEW THOUSAND MILES BETWEEN FRIENDS?

It started off rather casually,
just a penpal to write to oversea.
We seemed so different, didn't think it would last,
but we continued to write as time passed.

Valerie saved hard to come to my shore,
I was nervous wondering what was in store.
She was single and bright and loved Shakespeare,
I was wed, a mum who hated King Lear!

I envisaged her wearing gloves and pearls,
alighting from the bus in frilly swirls,
a volume of Shakespeare's tucked under arm,
exuding pure intellectual charm.

The jean-clad smiling lass I ignored,
and worriedly scanned the faces on board.
'Hi, I'm Valerie.' The myth was a dream,
the pearls and Shakespeare nowhere to be seen!

On paper we had seemed like cheese and chalk,
this disappeared when we began to talk.
Tastes and opinions we shared and agreed,
our friendship blossomed with amazing speed.

We are best friends across 6000 miles,
calls and tapes help us 'see' each other's smiles.
Problems and sadness, jokes and laughs we share,
like adopted sisters for each other we're there.

My family saved so hard to surprise me,
they paid for me to visit Valerie.
We toured so much it is beyond measure,
I have countless fond memories to treasure.

No matter that we are often apart,
My 'sister' always remains in my heart.

Linda Bagnall

OBSTRUCTION ON THE MOTORWAY

Dripping in diamonds, decked in fine gold,
wearing fine fashions by Mademoiselle Bold.
Champagne and oysters, truffles and wine -
a night at the opera, to make me feel fine.

I might use the Porsche - instead of the Jag,
the colour's not right, it will clash with my bag!
I'll summon the chauffeur, leave word with the cook -
if I'm not back by midnight, I hope she'll lock up.

It's Paris tomorrow in my private plane,
a little light shopping and lunch by the Seine.
My own dress designer, coiffeurs at a whim,
I'll hire Brighton beach, when I fancy a swim.

I'll start my world cruise on the Orient Express.
I'll shop 'til I drop in my gold lamé dress.
Men will adore me, we'll dine at the Ritz.
My life will be luxury, glamour and glitz.

I'll sleep in fine satins,
I'll feel like a queen.
When I wake up tomorrow -
will it all be a dream?

Will Saturday night's fever become a hot flush?
Will I still shop at Safeways and be in a rush?
Will life in the fast lane end up as a crawl?
Will I win the lottery, will my numbers fall?

Reality beckons and the washing-up waits,
the gravy's congealed as it's dried on the plates.
Six days of freedom and thoughts that are right -
I'll go on that cruise again - next Saturday night.

Audrey Woodall

Light Up A Light

Take time in your life to light up a light
Like a Christmas light it will shine big and bright
A Saviour was born on Christmas night
A baby, how beautiful, to bring us great light

A candle glows - with a flame big and bright
A light can glow - as well at night
But the light that glows from within our souls
Is the light of our Saviour who was born to save all

Remember that star - that beautiful star
That shone at great height - to bring shepherds at night
They brought great gifts to Jesus that night
An Angel appeared with the news that night

Christmas is jolly, Christmas is happy
But remember the birth of our Saviour that night
He was born to save all - to lighten up our hearts
At Christmas time - a light to shine

You look at your tree - at least lucky ones see
A beautiful sight - with lights shining bright
The joy of gifts around that tree
Bring happiness and joy for you and me

So remember at this time of our Dear Lord's birth
That it was Him that gave us this time on Earth
But with this message of love from me
I hope you kiss me under the mistletoe tree

Mary Jo West

DREAM GIVER

You wonderful dream giver,
Let me choose tonight.
Shall I float upon my bed to a distant land
Where I can forget what I have done today?
Carry me high, across the sky, floating
On the midnight breeze.
Let me feel the comforting warmth
And the carelessness of the darkened day.

Hurry along, my impatience grows.
Let me drift away to be a princess
Covered in sparkling jewels;
Or let me walk again with youthful steps
In an enchanting place;

And then, wonderful dream giver,
My mind will stop darting about,
And stop giving my tummy
That sinking pain of remembering.
Come to me tonight, don't betray me now,
For tomorrow I must pay
For what cannot be undone.

Doreen King

MISSING EWE

Memories of sheep's wool muffle my mind
Thick and scratchy and oily
Safe and familiar
Painfully familiar

I can't sleep for want of him
Count sheep? It's worth a try
One . . . he used to call me his innocent lamb
Now that innocence is shattered
Two . . . that one has his smile
Three . . . this isn't working

Excuse me? There's still BT!
And what ever happened to good old fashioned letters?

Dearest love,
I haven't been well.
Please come and visit me here. Please.
Bring your wheel and spindle.
Spin me a love that will keep my heart
Ever warm.

No! He must never know!
He must never know just how much
I miss his wool.

Naomi Engelkamp (15)

In My Thoughts

During the war I had a very dear friend
and I wonder if Poetry Now can reach her;
my thoughts are wafting in the wind
and may blow to her ear;
her name was Jean Wilsden,
she lived in Ascot
and worked for the Ministry of Supply,
I worked there too, in Leamington Spa,
she was a driver and I was on the telephones;
we were about twenty years old and
struck up a very strong friendship
straight away.
Her father worked for Kodak in Paris;
one evening, he took us both out for dinner.
I am remembering so many things now
and I hope, somehow, this will get to you
wherever you are.
You had lovely black curly hair
and wore royal blue and black a lot.
You were very pretty;
Oh! Jean if I could only meet
you again and
perhaps by a miracle this poem
will reach you.
You married a Czechoslovakian Officer;
he lost his leg in the war
and I remember, it was not a happy marriage.
Now I wonder where you are.
Maybe, my message will reach you in the wind,
because you are in my thoughts.

Irene Elliot

Winter Ploughing

The clouds scatter across the greying sky
Gently whipped by the soft wind,
But the sun is playing hide and seek in the heavens,
Shooting beams of winter light
Reflecting like mirrors
As they touch the shining steel blades of the plough
Hurling and thrusting their way
Through the dark sombre earth
To the screaming sounds of mob violence
As the seagulls dip and twist, soar and dive,
Their stark white and grey touched plumage
Highlighted against an ever darkening sky
As man in his droning machine
Trundles up and down the furrows,
Sedate - plodding - strong; -
In contrast, the sky is filled
With endless grace of movement
As the gulls continue to whirl and pivot,
Turning this winter scene
Into one glorious, joyous feeling of freedom.

Margaret Baxter

The Final Release

Cold-calloused concrete, and corroded iron bars,
form a dank, Medieval dungeon; from which there is but one inevitable
escape.

A sallow winter's sunset, sends the polluted tide of tourists ebbing
raucously away:
Leaving a wake of litter-strewn lawns,
and brimming cash tills.
And, for a brief, blessed moment; a tenuous air of peace.

Reflected in once-glorious eyes, the dying embers of a royal pride:
And a silent, anguished roar of protest.
But their gaze remains blurred, and unfocused:
Whilst an addled mind meanders, in hazy daydreams
of sweet, and poignant recollection.

Feebly, he shakes a mangy mane, in a final show of defiance.
As if to stir the mystic memories buried deep within him.
Memories of majestic, bygone age:
A time of space, and freedom.
Of endless, sun-dried horizons; where hot, summer winds
tease ochred dust-devils through the acacia.
And mercuried storm clouds peel away
to reveal a shining Eden.
Where the bold, new rays of life-light, spread
a satin-green sheen of youth across the plain:
Tempting home, a four-legged feast of abundance.

Bone-weary, the ancient captive sighs. Profoundly; helplessly:
Thankfully.
And eyes which once glittered with the fierce fires of topaz,
grow dim: Ephemeral spirit broken.
Slowly, they close one last time:
Never again to open.

The king is dead: But do not grieve.
At last, he is free: To flaunt, to gorge; to sun-doze.
To float timelessly, tirelessly, across those gilded plains.
Rejoice: The king is dead!
Long live the King!

Melanie Jane Banner

RGM

You were there that day
How many years ago?
You were there every day
Has it been that long?
From boys to men we grew together.
We learnt to read and write
We learnt to drive.
From games in the playground
To nights in a club.
And glasses of milk
To pints of beer.
Our lives are entwined forever
Those years can't be taken away.
You may not be here
But it cannot be changed.
Everything that's happened
We've been through together.
Only distance now separates us
Our friendship lives on.

Tim Hart

ONE NIGHT, LAST NIGHT

Not wanting to make a sound
I open my eyes and look around
Everything looks full of doom and gloom
Then I realise I am not in my bedroom.
My mind races to the night before
I remember, I was feeling low
I had a drink and then another
Trying to forget the fight with my lover
I turn around and look at you
Oh my God I still feel blue
Asking the question, how did I get here?
Think of an excuse and blame the beer
I know I will never feel the same
And I can't even remember your name
Watching your face, whilst you're asleep
I feel so dirty and cheap
What is everyone going to say
Probably something like, there goes an easy lay
Feeling my face go really red
I try to sneak out of bed.
You open your eyes and give out a laugh
Then I mutter I need a bath.
Running into the bathroom I hide away
Not hearing a single word you say
Looking in the mirror I am a sight
Oh no I have a love bite.
Running my fingers through my hair
All my confidence has been stripped bare
Today I should be wearing a wedding band
But I lost all that and got a one night stand.

Jacky Hartley

A One 'Knight' Stand

What about that man I saw?
Who stole my heart the night before,
The club was cosy, with lights so low
With drinks and laughter it did flow.

A man so handsome so it seemed
He was everything I had ever dreamed,
Sparkling eyes with promise filled
Any wonder I was so thrilled,

We danced so close heart to heart
As if our lives would never part,
And oh, it was such perfect bliss
Enhanced with every tender kiss.

Was this just a one night stand?
Had my heart got out of hand?
Was this my knight in armour clad?
Or in the morning would I be sad?

So precious was that special night
Too soon came cold mornings light,
Oh yes, I'm sad but regrets there's none
Because he will always be, my special one.

Pim Foster

APOPLECTIC!
(Dedicated to our son Mark placed 13,921 in 4:17:11)

N ew York, an Empire and Apple place;
E veryone is here to set the pace;
W onder who'll win this golden race.

Y ou're with the crowd, but on your own
O f course, a loneliness that's grown
R unning, pursuing; you must have known;
K eep going, ever onward, new seeds to be sown.

M anic desire, wanting to be done,
A ll this pain to be overcome.
R unning blind, looking but not seeing, numb,
A long the concrete, sun, run,
T owards the end, come on, don't be dumb;
H elp! Show me the way, chum, I'm
O ffering £sd to the Macmillan Fund. A
N ominated harrier now in the pits,
       who is thrilled to bits

                 in

           ninety six.

J A Wright

My Long Lost Cousin

I searched high and low
for your whereabouts
I wanted to know who I was
you were the missing key
Ever since I have discovered you
you are in my thoughts
of what ifs
my father has kept in touch
what then
even though we are far apart
the north and south divide
I have never stopped thinking
or loving you
although you have never been
part of my life
you are now
more than ever
even though we hardly know each other
you are there
that is all that matters
you are part of me and I in you
my dear cousin
may we never lose touch
if we do
do not grieve
we are there with each other
in spirit
and may the will of God
bring us forever closer

Susan Forrest

CHOICES

Take the road or fly the sky
Any way you choose,
Up and down and inside out,
Either way you lose.
Save the world or save yourself
the choice is yours alone
But what you do and what you say
Won't always lead you home.
Play the game, fight the war.
Take your cake and eat it.
Stand and watch or
          join the que.
Before you know it they're pushing you through
the system's got you.

Angela Watson

CONDOLENCES

My very dear friend at this sad time.
I had to write just a short line
To say that after the sorrow and pain,
the 'sun' will eventually shine again.

Remember that we care for you,
Take our love to see you through
Until the hurt becomes an ember
And only good times will you remember.

Carole Wallis

SHORELINE

If only you had waited
on the beach with me
you would have seen
the new-born light
cradled in the nursery
of the dawn
weaned into the full grown
chaos of the stressful day.

So now I wait alone
and watch the chattering waves
salting the morning air
as the impatient tide
surges into the submissive bay
where a lone gull shrieks
at the thrusting geese
who arrow the airways of the sky.

I wish that you were here
to see boats bobbing and dreaming
in their anchored harbour sleep
as gnarled old men
brown faced by sun and sea
talk endlessly of days long gone
remembering the ocean universe
deep dark and silver finned.

Stephen Gyles

BROWN STUDY

The name in sepia
Stares back 'cross forty years.
Hastening recall of days
When girls in uniform addressed others.

Through early years,
Letters flew and tokens of esteem.
Until young women laid pens aside
And took up service and Grenadiers.

Some broken homes and wholesome babies later,
Careers scorned by men who sighed for theirs.
Thoughts jelled, lost chances counted.
Exchanged and met, and theorised.

Be-ribboned airmail laid in secret drawers
Of desks piled high with bills, reports and legacies of life.
Address retrieved and brief explanations
Of tangled lives laid bare.
Brevity dictated by paper blue and colonial stamp.

Sufficient be it, that effort and the memory
Served put the whining thoughts of flight to bed.
And each glimpsed on reflection what might have been,
And lowered gaze on heightened colour at what they knew.

Barbara Turner

SEASONS

The seasons as a carpet spread
Not one can we honestly say we dread
All have there beauty to behold
As we watch them each unfold

Springtime is when they do say
That young lambs love to frisk and play
Young shoots from dormant earth doth sprout
And creatures from hibernation come out

Summertime is full and good
Hot days to wander through a wood
Through dapple leaves the sun shines down
The beauty of the trees in summer's gown

Autumn brings rich harvest time
Corn waving gold and smells divine
Fieldmouse and rabbit scamper away
To live elsewhere for a future day

Winter clothes the land in white
It truly is a wondrous sight
Long icicles from the roof tops hang
Across still night a carol sang

Hopeful for the return of spring
To start new seasons to begin
To sow, to crop, to reap
Our seasons that never sleep.

Joyce Boast

FIRST LOVE

It's a wonderful feeling,
A glow from within,
Spreads through your body,
Like a huge warming grin.
An inside out hug,
A heart in mid air,
A fluttering stomach,
A world without care.
A sense of great peace,
Like a single white dove,
A comforting thought,
It's a thing called first love.

A body that aches,
A head in cloud nine,
A wistful small glance,
That tells you he's mine.
A longing to see him,
A flush to the face,
A pounding inside of you,
Like winning a race.
A beautiful moment,
Sent to earth from above,
A small tender memory,
It's a thing called first love.

M Cook

Missing Out

Alarm is signalling
Time to move
A lazy stretch?
Not today,
get on your way

Breakfast ready
shovel it in
Friend for tea, mum?
Not today,
get on your way

Drop off the children
speed to work
have a nice day?
Not today,
get on your way

Type the letters
Answer the calls
School production?
Not today,
get on your way

Dash through the traffic
Home for tea
Children to the park?
Not today,
get on your way

Retired and lonely
Hours to spare
Play with the children?
Not today,
They've gone away.

Jayne Hempstock

AN IMMIGRANT'S FAREWELL

Farewell my friends, for I must leave you
And sail across the sea.
For home my heart is yearning,
My Scotland calls for me.

So it's back there I'm returning,
The land I love the best.
When my life on earth is done
It's there I'll be laid to rest.

No more will I wander no more will I roam
When once again again I see the shores,
That called out to me,
My dear old Scottish home.

I've travelled far through distant lands,
Since the day I left Scotia behind.
But it's back to my ain folks,
A welcome I will find.

Farewell my friends, God bless you all,
For me my memories there'll be,
As I travel back to Scotland.
That dear land across the sea.

David B Small

AN ACQUIRED TASTE

In a folk club one night in July '69,
You chatted me up and you smiled.
'Can I buy you a drink?' you asked boldly of me,
'Yes please, mine's a vodka and lime.'

But the glass you returned with was dimpled and fat,
And filled with brown liquid and froth.
'That's Tetley's Best Bitter,' you told me aghast,
As I started to splutter and cough.

'A taste that's acquired' you quickly assured.
But I doubted that your words were true.
So with a promise of wonders 'Double Diamond' you brought,
Followed quickly by a dark, creamy brew.

Nectar - some called it, as squinting they held,
The dark liquid up to the light.
Thoughtfully you watched, with a smile on your face,
As I tasted the black through the white.

As sheer disbelief quickly flooded my face,
Vodka you brought me in minutes.
But I said, 'Please don't bother for a taste I've acquired,
For a pint of this stuff they call Guinness.

Tess Thomas

LAST NIGHT OF THE POMS

Hotel's on front,
But room's at back
Won't be disturbed. Oh yeah?
You should have heard the frigging noise!

Flight at dawn,
Sozzled to bed for
Good night's sleep. Well -
You should have heard the frigging noise!

Street main passage to the front,
And from there
To all the universe -
You should have heard the frigging noise!

Cars come, trucks go
Mopeds, competing with mosquitoes
Whined us up all night -
You should have heard the frigging noise!

Is that a song I hear
From throats not parched
By any stretch of fevered imagination? -
You should have heard the frigging noise!

Low pitched rumblings
Underpin all this - low-tech freezers
In the kitchen just below, sub-sonic so to say -
You should have heard the frigging noise!

Last revellers sod off,
What a relief. Oh yes?
It's time to man the fishing boats -
You should have heard the frigging noise!

But - a pleasure to report
That we had our revenge -
On the noisiest bed springs in creation -
You should have heard the frigging noise!

Alan McAlpine Douglas

SUNDAY NIGHT

O wonderful beautiful
Sunday night
The evening you
Came and held me tight
Without any music
You danced with me
Then you sat and talked to me
You took me
Out of this earthly world
When you kissed me on Sunday night
Now we have said goodbye
And I know not the reason why
But I will wish and wish
With all my might
For another like
Sunday night

Marda Day

ABSENT MEMORIES

Do you see that young man there
- over there
The one in the middle
Well he sat here
Just here where I'm sitting right now

Oh it was a long time ago
Too long ago for him to remember
Of course he was never like that
When he sat here.

All that bravado laughter and life
Where's that going to get him

Look at him
Look at him now
- Oh he's just going up town
Gotta go - back later
- maybe -
        Ciaou

Well ciaou baby see you later
Me. - I'll still be here of course
Just here on this stool
Oh I'll be ok you needn't worry about me
What do I need to go up town for
I'm ok,
I'm ok just here.

Allen Meade

KATHLEEN

I walked home
With the taste
Of her lips
On my mouth
Feeling old
And foolish
And aroused.

Remembering
her body
Soft and sleek
In the sheets
Excited
While striding
Along the street.

Then wondered
What she thought
While stepping
Through the park
Of our love
And our lust
In the dark.

John Hopper

Renewal

'Our circumstances don't allow
Such great sadness in those words
We never question why or how
Freedom's just for frogs and birds

Or creatures dwelling by the streams
Free wild ponies graze their moors
All unaware of human dreams
Whom so do dream 'yond locked doors

Thus people build themselves a trap
In tethers of emotion
But always there, that tiny gap
In life's rich busy ocean

To see dear friends of long ago
The tears from memories linger
Those yearning hearts will sadly flow
As chores of life will hinder

Across the wires, we speak awhile
Substituting friendly hugs
Remembered whispers by the fire
Sipping coffee from large mugs

Sweet secrets shared, that joyous mirth
Memories cradled in one's mind
Those certain smiles, creating birth
Of friendship, love, 'twould ne'er unbind

Though many years have passed along
Very strange to say, but true
The friendship seemed to know no wrong
Unscathed by life's ugly hue

But ponder on - do spare a while
Life stands not still forever
Just take time out to stretch that mile
Make lifetime's wild endeavour

If meeting wishes come from both
That moment, jubilation.
'Twill add in years to further growth
Of memories past elation

Joyce Barbara

MUTUAL LOVE

So now you know me.
My thoughts,
My fears,
My past,
My outlook on life,
What makes me tick,
What makes me laugh.

We've learned so much
From just one night.
But yet this feels
Not quite right
A longing for love,
Not far away.
Has yet to pass.
Has yet to fade
So I can live, in today.

And this will end,
We'll go our ways.
Because I know,
You feel the same.

Scott Poulter

NIGHT FLIGHT

The beauty beneath me is breaking my heart,
as the steel-framed albatross roars aloft
over the vast, electric bulb-field
which is lit London, mystical as the Elysian
fields; for she is not with me to share,
to share the vision. So I will turn
my eyes upwards into blackness.

We parted with that momentary warmth of bodies,
lusciousness of final lips, mocked
by that notice - Passengers only beyond -
then, hand-luggaged, I swung away
into that lounge of chilled strangers.

Human caricatures are all around me,
loosening seat-belts, accepting beverages
and night socks from stewardesses, anticipating
jet-lag as we will plunge into a new world's
brisk today. Today will be tomorrow,
there, tomorrow and tomorrow a fantasy
of life with the only reality a dream,
a day-dream of her imagined presence.

Andrew Kerr

THE REBEL

Many years, many people, but none like you.
Young and so full of life, confident and sure,
My admiration was for your extrovert ways,
Seeing myself, a timid, lack lustre bore.

You did things that stretched my imagination,
Unconventional dress but you did not care,
Smoked sweet smelling cigarettes, so high!
Doing things, I could not, would not dare,

For all your outward easiness, there was,
A person who was very true, a loyal friend,
Never talking, without giving much more,
As reliable at the beginning, as you were at the end.

It's been many a year since we parted,
I often wondered what life you have now?
Will we ever meet again? I think out loudly,
What are you like? What do you do and how?

Are you still the rebel you were then?
Have you conformed and like me, turned grey?
Does the person I knew, still do her own thing?
Are you married, or still going your own way.

There may be, one day, who really knows?
In the not too distant future, when we,
Meet and talk of the days well remembered,
Of the people we once used to be.

Sheila Ellen Wright

BATTERSEA PARK

Do you remember the night you and I were locked inside
....Battersea Park?
We'd been walking and talking, so absorbed in each other, we
....didn't notice how dark
the night had become, that the people had gone and you and I
....were alone.
The last thing on our mind was the day or the time and the need
....for us both to get home.
Panic set in as we reached the park gates and found them locked
....for the night.
'What shall we do?' I cried out in dismay as you calmed me and
....held me so tight.
Then to make matters worse we heard thunder above as the sky
....was brightened by lightning.
Locked in the park in a storm in the dark - the situation was
....frightening!
We didn't have coats, umbrellas and such - young people in love
....never bother.
We thought we could weather wind, rain or storm as long as we had
....one another.
But that wasn't the case as I shivered and shook with the rain beating
....hard in my face.
It was like a bad dream - a real Halloween - we just had to get out of
....that place.
You set off to find a means of escape and I followed in gold
....strappy sandals,
praying hard that we'd find another park gate that may have been
....damaged by vandals.
We did find a gate but needless to say that one was locked tight
....as well.
But thank God you were tall, for high on the wall you found a
....security bell.
You pressed it so hard and rang it so long it seemed to go on for
....an age.
Ten minutes later the keeper arrived on the scene in a terrible rage!

He shouted and cursed which made us feel worse and really put us
                                                    in our place;
but he softened his tone when his torchlight shone on the teardrops
                                                    and rain on my face.
He unlocked the gate, sending us on our way with, 'Don't let it
                                                    happen again!'
As if we would want a repeat of that night in the park in the dark in
                                                            the rain.
We haven't met now for thirty-five years - both treading a
                                                    different path.
But do you find like me, when you think of that night, you smile
                                              first - then just have to laugh!

Valerie Dawson

FAMILY TIES

Once the house was full of noise
Children's voices, the rattle of toys
Baby crying, waiting to be fed
Joyful silence when they were all in bed.

Once the house was full of sound
Teenagers having their friends around
Windows shaking to the latest beat
Neighbours complaining across the street.

Once the house was full of laughter
Discos, parties, clearing up the day after
Then suddenly young love flew in the door
And my little terrors weren't mine any more.

Now the house is silent and still
Nothing but empty hours to fill
Waiting for a letter or a ring of the phone
Life is so lonely since the kids left home.

Jeanne Ellmore

Dwelling On A One Night Stand

Day breaks into the room,
Lights up the face of a man,
Terrible feelings and thoughts start to loom,
This is the face of a one night stand.

As I sit here looking at your face,
Thoughts of last night persecute my mind,
I need to escape get out of your place,
To leave all these feelings behind.

Regret soon hits, shame takes the lead,
How could it have happened with you?
Don't wake yet, I beg and I plead,
A lifetime of misery for a one night screw.

I leave my sixteen years on your pillow,
The thought of last night makes me cold,
Your fifty years of life really show,
Your look is weather beaten, worn and old.

I needed comfort, so you appealed last night,
Though only through much intoxication,
It was a mixture of drink and moonlight,
Charm, age and sophistication.

I've known you it seems like a lifetime,
That is why it is so hard to comprehend,
Against my father I feel we've committed a crime,
After all you are his lifelong best friend.

Kerry Brady

FRIENDSHIP STRAIGHT AND TRUE

Our friendship started long ago,
As colleagues in our work place,
We all went to a late night show,
Our work next day we could not face.

In our youth we were full of fun,
With lots of laughter through the day,
Our friendship grew since it begun,
We liked each other, by the way.

Then you announced your engagement,
And everyone was pleased for you,
Your wedding gifts and cards were sent,
With good luck wishes all life through.

You settled down with house and car,
With your partner, and three children,
And with promotion you went far,
It was all worthwhile to live then.

Our friendship lasted a long time,
It stayed quite thin, and yet quite strong,
I'm glad you are a friend of mine,
I knew that we would get along.

But now you have moved overseas,
And I feel left out of the fold,
We still send letters, and I'm pleased,
To have good memories of old.

I'm sure that we will meet again,
If we can recognise each other,
But times will never seem the same,
They'll never ever be recovered.

Doreen Ranson

INFORMATION

We hope you have enjoyed reading this book - and that you will continue to enjoy it in the coming years.

If you like reading and writing poetry drop us a line, or give us a call, and we'll send you a free information pack.

Write to :-

**Poetry Now Information
1-2 Wainman Road
Woodston
Peterborough
PE2 7BU**